what people are saying about this book

"Consuming a diet rich in plant foods is the best way to increase the health-protective substances called phytochemicals. This book makes it easy to implement these guidelines with its extensive list of foods and recipes designed around plant-centered cuisine."
— *Dr. Kenneth Cooper, founder, The Cooper Aerobics Center*

"Oh bliss! This book captures the joy of intensely flavored, interesting and wonderful food that brings health benefits as well. Food-lovers who are health-conscious must have this book."
— *Mary Abbott Hess, R.D., author of* The Healthy Gourmet Cookbook
and past president of the American Dietetic Association

"I like the common sense approach of *Phytopia*— the way the authors emphasize the sensual goodness of plants side by side with their nutritional virtues, all while keeping a portion of the meat that so many people are accustomed to eating. In particular, they do wonders for tofu, treating it with an open mind coupled with good ideas and badgering readers to do the same. We all need a little nudging to change our habits, and *Phytopia* provides not only the reasons to try, but the encouragement, information and tools to succeed."
— *Deborah Madison, author of* The Greens Cookbook *and*
Vegetarian Cooking for Everyone

"An inviting cookbook that transforms cutting-edge research into mouthwatering meals. Nutrition-minded readers will especially enjoy The Science Behind the Recipes."
— *Evelyn Tribole, R.D., author of* Healthy Homestyle Desserts *and*
former Good Morning America *nutritionist*

"*The Phytopia Cookbook* provides an excellent discussion of recent research findings upon which the recipes are based."
— *Gary Beecher, U.S. Department of Agriculture,*
Agricultural Research Service Food Composition Laboratory

D1305112

PHYTOPIA INC.
Dallas, Texas
(888) 750-9336

Library of Congress Catalog Card Number: 97-95067
Gollman, Barbara and Pierce, Kim.
The Phytopia Cookbook — A World of Plant-Centered Cuisine
by Barbara Gollman and Kim Pierce

Includes bibliographical references and index.
ISBN 0-9661875-4-7.

Cover illustration: David Povilaitis
Book design: Lesley Becker
Typesetting: Geckomedia

PHYTOPIA INC.
11705 Pine Forest Drive
Dallas, Texas 75230

A note to the reader: Nothing in this book should be construed as
a substitute for medical care or advice. The information is provided
for education only. Further, no one should undertake dramatic diet
or exercise changes without first consulting a physician.

the phytopia cookbook

A WORLD OF PLANT-CENTERED CUISINE

BY BARBARA GOLLMAN AND KIM PIERCE

about the authors

Barbara Gollman is a chef-trained registered dietitian and former medical microbiologist who grew up on a farm in Kansas. Good food was on the table every day — fresh cream and eggs, meat and potatoes, corn, tomatoes, pies and cakes. But her mother was such a perfectionist, Barbara wasn't encouraged to cook. Self-taught as an adult, she graduated from tuna-noodle casserole to course work at the Culinary Institute of America, Peter Kump's School of Culinary Arts and other culinary schools. A member of the International Association of Culinary Professionals and the American Dietetic Association, she teaches cooking, works with media on behalf of the American Dietetic Association and consults with restaurants.

Kim Pierce is an award-winning *Dallas Morning News* food journalist. Her love of cooking comes not from farm roots, but from growing up in the diverse ethnic swirl of Los Angeles. A member of the Association of Food Journalists and the American Institute of Wine and Food, she has written about food and studied cooking for almost 20 years, most recently at Johnson and Wales University.

table of contents

acknowledgments

For their unflagging support, encouragement, tireless effort and expertise, we especially thank Harvey Gollman and Phillip Bando. Also Rosina Wittmeyer, Ric Martin, Lesley Becker, David Povilaitis and Maggie.

For their extreme patience, we thank Anna Pierce and Tress Martin.

For their sweat, inspiration and ideas, a sympathetic ear or a ready kitchen, we thank Bill Marvel, Marty Kahn, Linda McDonald, Maureen Stanton, Lanette Causey, Tierney LaMaster, Teresa Gubbins, Lisa Ekus, Steve Steinberg, Maggi Manning, Deirdre Smith, Stella Bando, Sonya Calooy and Freddie Strange. And for her steadfastness and willingness to juggle schedule demands creatively, Cathy Barber.

For their attention to details that helped make this a better book, we are indebted to Kristi Steinmetz, Mary Abbott Hess, Ray Beecher and Lawrence Kushi.

And finally, we would like to thank Judith Jones, who helped us see that the science does belong behind the recipes, where it will not distract from the pleasure of the cuisine.

introduction

the phytopia name

You won't find "Phytopia" in any dictionary. It's a word we coined to describe the concept behind the cookbook. Combining "phyto," the Greek word for plant, with "utopia," *Phytopia* is the ultimate in plant-centered cuisine. Not the same as vegetarian, it nudges meat off the center of the plate to make room for more fruits, vegetables and grains. But not just plain fruits, vegetables and grains. *Phytopian* cuisine is first and foremost a feast for the senses that uses taste, texture, flavor, aroma and color to achieve the heights of pleasure and adventure one expects from great food.

the phytopia top 10

Here are some of the most powerful or promising phyto-foods:

Broccoli
Oranges
Garlic
Kale
Soybeans
Green tea
Red wine
Onions
Brussels sprouts
Tomatoes

If you have ever savored crème brûlée or a meltingly tender steak, chewy cheesy nachos or soup so rich it coats a spoon, you are passionate about food. You are a sensualist who relishes the pleasures of texture and taste. Were this not the case, it would be easy to sit down with brown rice and beans, steamed vegetables and bread — cheerless foods that, nonetheless, are good for you.

More than mere chewing and swallowing, eating is a gustatory celebration, and once you have partaken, it's hard to adopt monastic ways.

But the writing is on the kitchen wall. If your looks and health are important, you struggle with the knowledge that in so many ways we are what we eat. Today's butterfat expands tomorrow's thighs, or worse, constricts tomorrow's arteries. Six of the ten leading causes of death are diet-related and often specifically fat-related. These are premature deaths — death before one's natural time.

But between the extremes of Dionysian abandon and grim self-denial, there is a middle ground that promises enormous benefits while still delivering the deep satisfaction you've come to expect.

It's the world of *Phytopia*, a world of plant-centered cuisine whose fabulous flavors leap off the page. When our recipes are cooking, the wonderful aromas of garlic, rosemary, mint and lemon fill the air. Dishes like Tuscan Chicken, Greek Gazpacho and Bananas Diablo redefine our experience of flavor and seasoning. There may be no Alfredo sauce on a *Phytopian* plate. But it still engages the senses with a cascade of heady tastes, textures, aromas and colors.

the phytochemical revolution

Phytopian cuisine nudges meat to the side of the plate and gives fruits and vegetables more emphasis. The rationale comes from the relatively new field of phytochemical research. As forbidding as the word sounds, phytochemicals are nothing more than chemicals found in plants — "phyto" being the Greek word for plant. If you've heard of antioxidants, you're more familiar with phytochemicals than you may think: Like vitamins E and C and beta carotene, many phytochemicals have an antioxidant function. But there is so much more to phytochemicals. They are also the substances that make watermelon pink, cabbage stinky and wine full-bodied.

Across the spectrum, scientists are beginning to discover that phytochemicals may do amazing things in humans — like prevent cancer and heart disease, strengthen immunity and even slow aging. Not bad for a bunch of broccoli and onions. But much of the excitement hinges on the future promise from early research, especially lab and animal studies. This research portends considerable preventive and therapeutic benefits, and some phytochemicals have already progressed to human trials

— vitamin E, for example; the lesser-known limonene, found in orange peel oil; and controversial beta carotene.

Which means, in the coming months and years, you're going to hear and read more about individual phytochemicals such as lycopene, beta carotene, quercetin and genistein, as well as broad classes of compounds like carotenoids, phytosterols and flavonoids. As this research percolates into the popular press, it helps to remember that scientists look upon single studies as exchanges in an ongoing dialogue, not declarations of ultimate truth. It may be years, even decades, before something like a consensus is reached. Nevertheless, many in the field agree there's already solid evidence for the benefits of fruits and vegetables, based on hundreds of studies tracking the health of many kinds of people and what they eat. Taken together, these studies indicate that a diet rich in fruits, vegetables and grains enhances your odds for a longer, more healthful life.

For those wishing to learn more about phytochemicals, we have condensed hundreds of studies and other materials into a comprehensive primer that outlines the research, defines terms and lists the phytochemicals in individual foods. It's The Science Behind the Recipes, which starts on Page 135.

But even if you never crack the science section, you can still enjoy the benefits of plant-centered cuisine just by eating the *Phytopian* way.

foods of the sun

Plant-centered means just that: Bringing fruits, vegetables and grains to the center of the plate without necessarily forsaking meat and other higher-fat pleasures. Plant-centered cuisine simply moves these to the periphery and uses them differently. The goal is vegetables, fruits and grains so delicious and compelling, so irresistible, that you never miss the meats and fats they replace. (And you will end up replacing, to some degree, as opposed to adding on — unless you want to add on extra pounds.)

Not surprisingly, *Phytopian* cuisine is inspired by sunny climes — the Mediterranean, Southeast Asia and the American Southwest — where so many plant foods flourish: From Morocco, fruited chicken braised atop a spiced melange of onions, kumquats, prunes, honey and squash. A spicy Thai salad that starts with layers of cabbage, basil, red onion, carrot and radish tossed in tangy chile-lime dressing. Hot Potatoes With Corn and Poblanos that evokes the flavors of the mesa. Other *Phytopian* dishes are inspired by the California sun: Chicken roulade stuffed with spinach and goat cheese over warm greens. Or Turkey-Watercress Burgers, a most unorthodox blend of ingredients that produces an incredibly moist and meaty flavor rush.

Phytopian food entices with colors and aromas as much as with

the phytopia pantry

Here are some of the ingredients to keep on hand for making the recipes.

the pantry shelf:

Anchovy paste
Asian fish sauce
Beans, canned: black
Bulgur
Capers
Chicken broth, nonfat
  and reduced-sodium
Couscous
Garlic
Ginger
Horseradish
Kitchen Bouquet
Mustards: Creole,
  Dijon
Nonstick cooking
  spray: butter flavor
  and olive oil flavor
Nuts: almonds, pine
  nuts, walnuts and
  pecans
Oils: canola, walnut,
  sesame and other
  nut oils
Olive oil: extra virgin,
  and flavored, if
  desired
Rice: brown (regular
  or parboiled), bas-
  mati or jasmine
Sesame seeds

Sherry, cream
Tofu: light, firm and
    extra firm
Tomatoes, canned
Tomato juice or V-8
Vermouth
Vinegars: red wine,
    balsamic, rice and
    sherry wine
Worcestershire sauce

the spice rack:

Allspice
Basil
Bay leaves
Cardamom, ground
Cayenne pepper
Chili powder
Cinnamon
Cloves, whole and
    ground
Coriander, ground
Cumin, ground and
    whole
Fennel seed
Ginger, ground
Mustard, whole seeds
    and dry
Nutmeg
Oregano
Peppercorns: white,
    black and pink
Red pepper flakes
Rosemary
Tarragon
Turmeric
Thyme

in the freezer:

Apple juice
    concentrate
Grape juice
    concentrate
Orange juice
    concentrate

flavors. With few exceptions (Chile-Rubbed Pan-Fried Chicken is down-right ugly), these dishes blaze with color — luscious tomato and bell pepper reds, glistening spinach and lettuce greens, brilliant turmeric and corn yellows, hints of pink-purple from raspberry and blueberry.

Dessert is probably the most expendable course where your body's well-being is concerned. But not your psyche. Too nourishing in subtle ways, too important to sacrifice. In the Mediterranean Diet, about which so much has been written, intangibles such as communal aspects of life — sharing food as a social activity, resting after the midday meal — are suspected of playing a role in the people's vibrant good health. And so, in the same spirit, we cannot dismiss dessert.

But whether dessert or pizza, flavor is paramount. We love the way grilling and roasting coax out flavors. Herbs, mustard, citrus and chiles are bedrock "big" flavoring ingredients. But we also use higher-fat foods such as assertively flavored cheeses to bring out the best in fruits, vegetables and grains. Also olive oil and walnut oil. Even butter. Paradoxically, fat may not matter in the way we think it does. In some studies, people with long, relatively disease-free lives ate as much fat as the average American. But they ate more fruits and vegetables, less meat and almost no animal fat. Newer studies also suggest the type of fat may be important.

Physical activity also figures into the equation, and any book about eating and health — even a cookbook — would be remiss in not pointing out its importance in a long and vibrant life. Health experts agree that regular, moderate physical activity is essential. Not only does it benefit the heart, it may also play a role in cancer prevention. Wine is another factor, but the voices are more cautionary, the benefits more clouded. Moderate amounts — one glass a day for women, two for men — appear to be heart protective. Beyond lies increased cancer risk.

the new road taken

Some of the recipes in this book can look daunting — especially the main dish salads. But these beautiful, intensely satisfying salads replace entire meals, so it follows that they require longer to prepare than traditional salads. A better comparison might be the time you would spend fixing meat, potatoes and vegetable. It's also possible to make some components ahead, such as the Bulgur Salad with Sun-Dried Tomatoes, Basil and Almonds that's part of the main-dish Hearty Mediterranean Salad. Convenience products can also trim prep time; we encourage the use of pre-cut greens and other salad ingredients, pre-cooked chicken or shrimp and parboiled brown rice, which requires 10 minutes to cook.

Once you've made a few of these main dish salads, which start with an imaginatively dressed bed of greens, you'll want to adapt the

strategy to your own favorite ingredients. If these include a creamy
dressing, consider replacing some of the fat with blended tofu.

Tofu? *Tofu?*

If ever an ingredient shouted "anti-gourmet," it is tofu — at least
in this country. But before turning up your nose or rolling your eyes,
hear us out. We won't belabor the considerable benefits; they're in The
Science Behind the Recipes. But because soyfoods are so integral to
plant-centered cuisine, we felt compelled to find ways of including them.

Then a funny thing happened. The more we experimented in the
kitchen, the more we discovered unique cooking properties — characteristics that make tofu more than a "health food" ingredient. Take blended
tofu (tofu whipped in a small food processor or blender). The texture is a
cross between salad dressing and cream cheese, yet the flavor is transparent. This does not mean benign like flour or cream. In the presence of
certain ingredients, notably garlic, blended tofu amplifies flavor, kicking
it up to amazing strength. In the presence of other flavors, like those in
Very Berry Swirl, tofu's a leveler. In custard, it becomes egglike, replacing some of the fat without sacrificing richness. It even works in sauces,
as in Creamy Lemon Orzo — a dish no one would suspect is tofu-based.
Take it home in a plain brown wrapper, if you must. But give tofu a
chance. Allow yourself to be pleasantly surprised.

We venture even further into the health-food sphere with tempeh,
another soy product. We won't even try to explain, except to say that in
the Moroccan Tajine it adds a pleasing meaty presence.

There's no escaping the health-foodie overtones of plant-centered
cuisine. Whole grains, fresh fruits and vegetables and tofu are clearly
crossover concepts. The difference is orientation. One speaks of health
food, with the emphasis on health. We speak of plant-centered cuisine
with the emphasis on cuisine. Not that there aren't lots of good-tasting
health foods. It's just that in the years since its popularization, people
have been willing to sacrifice some gustatory pleasure for the sake of
well-being. The point of plant-centered cuisine is flavor first.

*****

When we began writing, we told a globe-trotting gourmet cook
that the book was about healthy gourmet cooking. He smiled and said,
"Isn't that an oxymoron?"

To which we reply: Not if you understand flavor and seasoning.
Not if you know what you're doing in the kitchen. Not in the world
of *Phytopia*.

phytopia techniques

Here are techniques for preparing different ingredients called for throughout the book:

Blending tofu: Whip tofu in a small food processor or blender until it reaches the consistency of mayonnaise. Alternatively, whip with a hand blender. (A handheld electric mixer won't work.) Be patient: It takes several minutes to reach the proper consistency. Store tightly covered in the refrigerator up to one week.

Toasting nuts or seeds: Preheat oven to 400° F. Evenly spread nuts or seeds over the bottom of a baking pan. Check after 5 minutes and shake or stir. If nuts are just starting to color, leave about 1 minute more, until golden. Remove nuts from pan immediately, or they will continue cooking. Toasted seeds and nuts may be frozen in zip-top bags for several months. You can also toast them in a small skillet over medium heat, shaking the pan occasionally.

Making chiffonade of basil: Wash and dry leaves. (A salad spinner works well.) Stack leaves, starting with the largest leaf on the bottom and finishing with the smallest one on top. Start at one long edge of the bottom leaf and roll tight, like a cigar. With a sharp knife, slice across the roll, making very thin slices, until all the basil is sliced.

Roasting corn: Roast corn in husks at 450° F for 25 minutes. Remove from oven and set aside until cool enough to handle. Starting at the top, pull husks and silks down until ear is exposed; pull off husks and discard. Stand ear on end on a cutting board. Using a sharp or serrated knife, cut off kernels close to the cob from top to bottom. The corn can be refrigerated or frozen in zip-top bags.

Peeling an orange with a knife: Cut the top and bottom off the orange horizontally. Set orange, flat side down, on cutting board. Starting at the top, slice downward as close the fruit as possible, following the contour of the fruit, removing peel and white membrane completely.

Peeling and cubing a mango: Locate the stem end and the flat side of the mango; stand the mango with the stem end up. Place the blade of a sharp knife parallel to the flat side about ½ inch from the stem and slice from top to bottom. Repeat with other flat side. Place one half, skin side down, on the cutting board. With the tip of your knife, score the mango flesh into cubes the size you need. Now, hold one end in each hand and "pop" the side inside-out, so the cubes stand up and separate. Cut cubes off close to the skin. Repeat with second half. Remove remaining "sides" from mango, cut away skin and cube.

about the nutritional analysis

Because the nutrient content of foods varies depending on growing conditions, season, transit time to market and other factors, the nutritional analyses with the recipes are, at best, estimated values. Optional ingredients are not included. In recipes where the serving size is expressed as a range, the analyses reflect an average: A dish that serves four to six, for example, is calculated for five servings. In recipes calling for "salt to taste," no added salt has been included in the analyses.

the value of good food

We think nothing of paying several dollars a pound for chicken breasts or pork chops. But we blanch at tomatoes for $3 a pound or lettuce at $2. In this culture, we've been taught to value meat for its protein and to devalue fruits and vegetables.

In the years before World War II, when many Americans were malnourished, emphasizing protein was important. But today, when we are much more likely to overconsume protein, such emphasis makes little sense.

Yet old habits and beliefs die hard. If we can begin to look upon fruits and vegetables as the new harbingers of good health, perhaps they will not seem quite so expensive.

In addition, you can control cost as well as enjoy the most flavorful produce by using what's in season locally. Shorter transit time from farm to market increases the odds that fruits and vegetables are picked ripe or nearly ripe. Vine-ripe berries are sumptuous in the Pacific Northwest. In season, Georgia peaches are pure nectar. Fresh off the stalk corn needs no salt or butter. And fresh, vine-ripe tomatoes bear no resemblance to their mealy counterparts that travel overland to market.

If it isn't possible to take advantage of local produce, become an educated consumer so you know the freshest, best-tasting produce on any given day at the supermarket. Chat up the produce manager; most are flattered by your interest and happy to talk with an informed, curious consumer.

soups & stews

soups & stews

When a soup or stew is simmering on the stove, aromas waft into every nook, filling the house with anticipation. Onion and garlic permeate the air, entwined with the gentle scent of herbs — basil, oregano, perhaps mint. If it's Osso Bucco-Style Stew, wine and meaty broth overtones mingle in the air. If it's Uptown Louisiana Gumbo, the nutlike smell of toasted flour signals the arrival of the bayou's holy trinity: sizzling onion, celery and bell pepper. These soups and stews warm us like the hearth where they traditionally simmer. Of course, not all soups are cool-weather hearty. Greek Gazpacho unites the sunny flavors of tomatoes, cucumbers, olives and feta. Very Berry Swirl is creamy and cooling. Recipes in this chapter do have one thing in common: All strategically deepen and expand flavors, whether by searing spices or braising. That they are healthful comes as a bonus.

mediterranean lentil ragoût

Orange juice gives this savory stew depth, and mint adds cooling freshness. This is a tasty introduction to some of the more exotic grains, such as quinoa and bulgur.

Olive oil cooking spray

1 large onion, finely chopped

5 cloves garlic, finely minced

1 jalapeño pepper, finely minced

1 large fennel bulb, sliced thin

1 (28-ounce) can diced tomatoes

1½ cups orange juice

1⅓ cups lentils, picked over and rinsed

1 tablespoon dried basil

1 tablespoon dried oregano

¼ cup tomato paste

⅓ cup mint leaves, chopped (divided use)

6 cups cooked rice, quinoa or bulgur

Parmesan cheese (optional)

Pre-prep: Cook rice, quinoa or bulgur. Chop onion; mince garlic and jalapeño; slice fennel bulb; chop mint.

1. Spray a heavy skillet cooking spray; place over low heat and sauté onion, garlic, jalapeño and fennel, stirring occasionally, until soft, about 5 minutes. (If vegetables start to stick or brown, cover skillet.)

2. Add tomatoes, orange juice, lentils, basil, oregano and tomato paste. Increase heat and bring to a boil. Reduce heat, cover, and simmer for 40 to 50 minutes, or until lentils are tender. (Add up to ½ cup water or orange juice if ragout gets too thick.)

3. Stir in mint leaves, reserving 2 tablespoons for garnish. Serve lentil stew over rice, quinoa or bulgur. Garnish with Parmesan cheese, if using, and remaining chopped mint.

Serves 6

Each serving has approximately:

Cals: 449	*Sodium: 367 mg*	*Calcium: 112 mg*
Total fat: 2.4 g	*Chol: None*	*Carbs: 88 g*
Sat fat: 0.4 g	*Fiber: 19 g*	*Protein: 20 g*

soups & stews

osso bucco-style stew

Meat-eaters love this hearty dish that satisfies like the real thing. There's no skimping on richness, yet replacing some of the veal with mushrooms keeps the dish from being so meat-intense.

Olive oil cooking spray

1 tablespoon olive oil

¼ cup flour

½ teaspoon salt plus black pepper to taste

1 pound lean veal stew meat, well trimmed of fat, cut into ¾-inch cubes

1 large yellow onion, diced

1 leek, white part only, diced (optional)

4 cloves garlic, chopped (divided use)

¾ cup dry red wine

2 cups beef broth

3 tablespoons tomato paste

½ teaspoon dried basil

½ teaspoon dried oregano

¾ pound mushrooms, cleaned and quartered

½ cup chopped flat leaf parsley

Grated peel of 1 lemon

Pre-prep: Trim and cube veal; dice onion; rinse leek thoroughly and dice, if using; chop garlic, parsley; clean and quarter mushrooms; grate lemon peel.

1. Preheat oven to 325° F. Spray a large nonstick oven-proof skillet with cooking spray and place over medium-high heat; add olive oil. Mix flour, salt and pepper in a plastic bag; add veal cubes and shake to coat all sides. Add meat to hot skillet, reduce heat to medium; cook, stirring often, until all sides of the cubes are browned. Remove meat from skillet and reserve. It's OK if the meat does not appear well cooked.

2. Add the onions, leek, if using, and half the garlic to the skillet. Stir to remove browned bits from skillet bottom. Reduce heat and cover, stirring occasionally, until onion is light brown.

3. Stir in the wine, beef broth and tomato paste. Stir in the browned meat, basil and oregano. Increase heat to high and bring to a boil. Cover, place skillet in the oven and braise for 1½ hours. Add mushrooms; simmer ½ hour longer, uncovered.

4. Just before serving, add remaining garlic, parsley and grated lemon peel.

Serves 6

Each serving has approximately:

Cals: 298	*Sodium: 601 mg*	*Calcium: 59 mg*
Total fat: 10.3 g	*Chol: 95 mg*	*Carbs: 17 g*
Sat fat: 2.4 g	*Fiber: 2 g*	*Protein: 29 g*

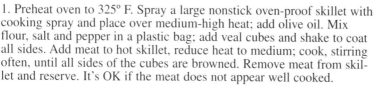

moroccan tajine

Tempeh, with its transparent flavor and nutlike texture, adds a meaty dimension to this mellow, colorful Middle Eastern stew. Serve it with Fruited Couscous made with prunes, which add surprising richness. No snickering.

Olive oil cooking spray

1 tablespoon cinnamon

½ teaspoon turmeric

1 teaspoon ground cumin

1 teaspoon coriander

1 large onion, diced

4 cloves garlic, minced

1 tablespoon minced ginger

1 (8-ounce) package wild rice-flavored tempeh, cubed

2 to 3 (14.5-ounce) cans diced tomatoes, or whole, chopped tomatoes with juice (see note)

3 large carrots, cut in ¼-inch coins

3 stalks celery, cut in ½-inch pieces

1 large turnip, peeled, cut in ½-inch cubes (optional)

1 lemon, sliced in rounds

2 cups cauliflower florets or 3 medium zucchini, cut in ½-inch cubes

1 tablespoon honey

Salt to taste

2 tablespoons minced cilantro

3 tablespoons pine nuts, toasted (See Page 17)

Harissa sauce (see note)

Pre-prep: Dice onion; mince garlic, ginger, cilantro; cube tempeh; slice carrots and celery; peel and cube turnip; slice lemon; separate cauliflower into florets or cube zucchini; toast pine nuts (see Page 17).

1. Spray a large Dutch oven with cooking spray and place over low heat. Add cinnamon, turmeric, cumin and coriander. Stir spices until fragrant, about 2 minutes. Add onion, garlic and ginger; increase heat to medium and sauté about 3 minutes. (Cover if vegetables start to stick.)

2. Meanwhile, place enough water in a small saucepan to cover the cubed tempeh, but don't add the tempeh yet. Bring water to a boil, add tempeh and cook 5 minutes. Drain well.

3. To the Dutch oven, add tomatoes, carrots, celery, turnip, if using, and lemon slices. Cover and simmer about 10 minutes. Add the cauliflower or zucchini and tempeh; simmer 10 to 15 minutes, until all vegetables are tender. Remove and discard lemon rounds. Add honey and salt to taste. Garnish with cilantro and pine nuts; serve with harissa sauce (see note).

Serves 6

Each serving has approximately:

Cals: 200	Sodium: 391 mg	Calcium: 122 mg
Total fat: 5.6 g	Chol: None	Carbs: 30 g
Sat fat: 0.8 g	Fiber: 9 g	Protein: 12 g

note

Use 2 or 3 cans of tomatoes, depending on whether you prefer a lot of liquid or just a little. You can use a different hot sauce, but harissa, a Middle Eastern chile condiment available in Middle Eastern and many gourmet stores, is made to complement these flavors.

tip

Terrified of tempeh? Despite its health-foodie-sounding name, this ingredient is very user-friendly. Found in the frozen food case at natural foods stores, it is a fermented soy product that has a slightly chewy texture like walnuts or pecans and a mild, neutral taste like mushrooms. It defrosts in about two minutes in the microwave and loves a marinade.

greek gazpacho

This soup wraps the flavors of a Greek salad into a cool gazpacho — right down to bits of Kalamata olives and feta cheese.

2 cups tomato juice (divided use)

Juice of 1 lemon

1 to 2 cloves garlic, peeled

2 tablespoons fresh oregano, leaves only, or 2 teaspoons dried

1 cucumber, peeled, seeded and roughly chopped

½ yellow or red onion, roughly chopped

12 Kalamata olives, pitted and rinsed (divided use)

1 tablespoon extra-virgin olive oil

1 ounce feta cheese, crumbled

4 teaspoons chopped parsley (optional)

Pre-prep: Juice lemon; peel garlic cloves; pick oregano leaves from stems; peel, seed and chop cucumber; chop onion; pit Kalamatas if you don't buy them that way, chop and reserve 4 or 5 for garnish; chop parsley, if using.

1. Place 1 cup tomato juice, the lemon juice, garlic and oregano in a blender or food processor. Pulse just to pulverize.

2. Add remaining tomato juice, cucumber, onion, olives and olive oil. Pulse (about 8 times) to chop vegetables. Swirl in crumbled feta and parsley, if desired. Serve cold or at room temperature; sprinkle each serving with chopped olives. The flavor improves overnight in the refrigerator; the onion especially pops out.

Serves 4-6

Each serving has approximately:

Cals: 83	*Sodium: 433*	*Calcium: 66 mg*
Total fat: 5.3 g	*Chol: 5 mg*	*Carbs: 8 g*
Sat fat: 1.4 g	*Fiber: 2 g*	*Protein: 2 g*

tangy tomato–fish stew

Say "fish stew" and most people turn up their noses. But this fresh-tasting stew is so beguiling, even a 12-year-old all-American Rollerblader pronounced it delicious — after picking out the onions.

¾ pounds halibut, fresh or thawed

1½ onions, chopped (divided use)

1 tablespoon butter

Juice of 3 lemons (divided use)

1 teaspoon olive oil

1 (10-ounce) can chopped tomatoes and chiles

1 (15-ounce) can chopped tomatoes, no salt added

1 (14½-ounce) can low-sodium chicken broth

½ teaspoon salt or to taste

2 tablespoons cilantro or parsley, minced

Pre-prep: Chop onions; juice lemons; mince cilantro or parsley.

1. Preheat oven to 350° F. Place fish in a oven-proof glass dish. Top fish with ¾ cup chopped onions; dot with butter, cut into 6 pieces. Drizzle with 3 tablespoons lemon juice. Bake 30 minutes, uncovered. If bottom of dish becomes dry, add a little water.

2. Meanwhile, add oil to a large saucepan over medium-high heat. Add remaining onions and cook just until they begin to caramelize, stirring only occasionally. Stir in canned ingredients; bring to a simmer and lower heat.

3. Remove fish from oven. Trim away and discard skin, bones and dark flesh. Roughly flake the fish in the cooking dish and scrape up any browned bits that may be on the bottom of the dish. Add to simmering liquid. Add remaining lemon juice and salt.

4. Return to a simmer for about 5 minutes. Will hold on very low heat for up to one-half hour. Serve with cilantro or parsley garnish.

Serves 4

Each serving has approximately:

Cals: 207	*Sodium: 400 mg*	*Calcium: 106 mg*
Total fat: 7.1 g	*Chol: 36 mg*	*Carbs: 16 g*
Sat fat: 2.7 g	*Fiber: 3 g*	*Protein: 21 g*

soups & stews

thai hot and sour soup

Chiles and lime juice give this light summer soup its hot-and-sour zip. Use the Thai chiles and it will make you sweat — natural air-conditioning for hot climates.

8 cups chicken stock or 4 (16-ounce) cans reduced-sodium, fat-free chicken broth

3 stalks lemon grass, cut into 1-inch pieces

2 limes (see Pre-prep)

2 serrano or jalapeño chiles, sliced lengthwise

8 ounces boneless, skinless chicken breast, cut into ¾-inch cubes

2 tablespoons Asian fish sauce

1½ cups bean sprouts

1 cup pineapple tidbits, drained

4 small Roma tomatoes, quartered

2 very hot Thai chiles (optional, see note)

2 tablespoons cilantro leaves, coarsely chopped

4 green onions, sliced

Pre-prep: Peel lemon grass and cut into 1-inch pieces; slice chiles; cube chicken; quarter tomatoes; chop cilantro; slice onions. To prepare limes: Remove the peel from 1 lime with vegetable peeler; coarsely chop. Squeeze juice from both limes into a small bowl.

1. Place chicken broth, lemon grass, minced lime peel and serrano chiles in large non-reactive saucepan over medium-high heat. Bring to a boil, cover and reduce heat; simmer for 20 minutes.

2. Strain out solids and return broth to saucepan; increase heat and bring to boiling. Add the chicken, fish sauce, lime juice, bean sprouts, pineapple, tomatoes and Thai chiles, if using. Stir and heat gently for 2 minutes until chicken is cooked.

3. Remove and discard Thai chiles. Garnish each bowl of soup with cilantro and green onions.

Serves 6

Each serving has approximately:

Cals: 114	*Sodium: 539 mg*	*Calcium: 70 mg*
Total fat: 1 g	*Chol: 15 mg*	*Carbs: 10 g*
Sat fat: 0.2 g	*Fiber: 2 g*	*Protein: 15 g*

note

Thai chiles can be found at Asian food stores and in the produce section of some grocery stores.

tip

Sour power: Soften hard limes and lemons in the microwave by heating on Low (30% power) for 1 minute to "ripen." Don't pierce them first — they will leak!

soups & stews

smoky southwestern vegetable soup

This wonderfully chunky, chile-laced soup gets its smokiness not from the chicken but from chipotle chiles.

2 dried chipotle chiles, stems and seeds removed

1 large onion, peeled, cut into 8 pieces

2 celery stalks, cut into 2-inch pieces

1 leek, white part only, cut into 2-inch pieces

1 poblano pepper, quartered

1/2 red bell pepper, cut in half

Olive oil cooking spray

1 (46-ounce) can V-8 Lightly Tangy Vegetable Juice (divided use)

1 turnip, peeled and coarsely chopped or grated

10 tomatillos, husks removed, coarsely chopped

1/4 teaspoon grated lemon peel

8 ounces smoked chicken or turkey, chopped (see note)

1 (16-ounce) can black beans, drained and rinsed

1 cup corn, fresh or frozen

2 limes, quartered

1/4 cup finely minced cilantro

Pre-prep: Stem and seed chipotle chiles; chop vegetables; peel and chop or grate turnip; husk and chop tomatillos; grate lemon peel; chop chicken or turkey; drain and rinse beans; mince cilantro.

1. In a small food processor or spice grinder, pulverize chipotle chiles. Set aside.

2. In a large food processor bowl, place onion, celery, leek, poblano pepper and bell pepper. Pulse until evenly minced.

3. Coat a large kettle or stockpot with olive oil cooking spray and place over medium-high heat. Add the chopped vegetables and about 1/4 cup of V-8; cook the vegetables, stirring, until soft, about 7 minutes.

4. Add remaining juice, 1 teaspoon of ground chipotle chile, turnip, tomatillos, lemon peel and chicken or turkey. Lower heat, cover and simmer 1 hour. (Reserve any remaining chipotle for another use.)

5. Add beans and corn; simmer until heated. Serve with lime quarters and cilantro.

Serves 6

Each serving has approximately:

Cals: 227	*Sodium: 678 mg*	*Calcium: 111 mg*
Total fat: 1.2 g	*Chol: 22 mg*	*Carbs: 41 g*
Sat fat: 0.2 g	*Fiber: 8 g*	*Protein: 17 g*

note

The heat of the chipotles will increase as the soup ages.
For meat, you can use smoked turkey from the deli cut in 1/2-inch pieces.

soups & stews

uptown louisiana gumbo

A cold-weather belly-pleaser, especially after a run on the slopes. Have two servings; it won't slow you down.

¼ cup all-purpose flour

Olive oil cooking spray

1 large onion, chopped

1 large red or green bell pepper, diced

1 stalk celery, minced

4 cloves garlic, minced

4 cups nonfat, reduced-sodium chicken broth

1 (28-ounce) can crushed tomatoes with puree

2 cups okra pods, trimmed, cut into ½-inch pieces

½ teaspoon freshly ground black pepper

¼ teaspoon dried thyme

¼ teaspoon dried oregano

⅛ teaspoon cayenne pepper

1 bay leaf

½ cup long grain, brown or basmati rice (see note)

6 ounces medium shrimp, peeled and deveined, or crabmeat

5 ounces boneless, skinless chicken breast, cut in ½-inch cubes

2 ounces turkey or chicken Italian sausage, crumbled

Salt to taste

Hot pepper sauce to taste

Pre-prep: Chop onion, pepper, celery and garlic; cut okra; peel and devein shrimp; cube chicken breast; remove sausage from casing and crumble.

1. Toast flour in 400° F oven for 20 minutes (see note). Spray a heavy stockpot with cooking spray; place over medium heat and sauté onions, bell peppers, celery and garlic for about 7 minutes. Stir in toasted flour.

2. Gradually add chicken broth and bring to a simmer, stirring. Add tomatoes, okra, pepper, thyme, oregano, cayenne and bay leaf. Cover and simmer for 15 minutes.

3. Stir in rice; continue to simmer for 25 minutes longer (see note). Test rice before adding remaining ingredients; it should be almost done. Then add the shrimp or crabmeat, chicken and sausage. Simmer 5 minutes longer or until shrimp is opaque, chicken is firm and rice is tender. Add salt and hot pepper sauce to taste.

Serves 6

Each serving has approximately:

Cals: 199	*Sodium: 250 mg*	*Calcium: 79 mg*
Total fat: 3.1 g	*Chol: 61 mg*	*Carbs: 27 g*
Sat fat: 1.1g	*Fiber: 2.4 g*	*Protein: 16 g*

note

Toasting the flour omits the need for a traditional roux, a source of considerable fat in gumbos. Flour toasts faster in a metal pan; remove flour from the oven when it looks tan and smells like burning toast.

If using brown rice in this recipe, increase cooking time to 40 minutes and test for doneness.

soups & stews

turkey tomatillo chili

Not for the faint of heart, this is a man's chili — meaty, hot and big-flavored.

2 whole dried chipotle chiles, stems and seeds removed

1 pound fresh tomatillos, husks removed, rinsed well

Olive oil cooking spray

1 large onion, chopped

6 cloves garlic, minced (divided use)

1 tablespoon ground cumin

1¼ pounds ground turkey breast

1½ cups fat-free chicken broth

1 bay leaf

1 teaspoon salt or to taste

1½ teaspoons dried oregano, crumbled

1 red bell pepper, chopped

2 (4-ounce) cans mild green chiles, drained and chopped

1 tablespoon cornmeal

1 (16-ounce) can black beans, rinsed and drained

½ cup plus 2 tablespoons chopped cilantro (divided use)

1 cup nonfat yogurt

Pre-prep: Stem and seed chipotles; husk and rinse tomatillos; chop onion, bell pepper, green chiles, cilantro; mince garlic; rinse and drain beans.

1. Soak chipotle chiles in 1 cup boiling water for 20 minutes, then puree in a small food processor with 1 to 2 tablespoons of the soaking liquid; set aside.

2. Blanch tomatillos in boiling water for 5 minutes. Puree in a food processor or blender and reserve.

3. Spray a large kettle with cooking spray and place over medium heat. Add the onions and half the garlic and cook, stirring, until softened. Add the cumin, stir for 30 seconds, then add the turkey. Continue to cook and stir, breaking up the turkey chunks.

4. When turkey is no longer pink, add the chipotle puree and tomatillo puree, broth, bay leaf, salt and oregano. Lower heat and simmer, uncovered, for 1 hour.

5. Stir in the bell pepper, green chiles and cornmeal. Simmer, with occasional stirring, for 30 minutes. Stir in the beans, ½ cup cilantro and remaining garlic; heat 3 to 5 minutes longer. Discard bay leaf.

6. Stir the remaining cilantro into the yogurt and add a dollop to garnish each serving of chili.

Serves 6

Each serving has approximately:

Cals: 301　　*Sodium: 803 mg*　　*Calcium: 177 mg*
Total Fat: 9.1 g　　*Chol: 75 mg*　　*Carbs: 28 g*
Sat Fat: 2.2 g　　*Fiber: 6.8 g*　　*Protein: 27 g*

Soups & stews

very berry swirl

Enjoy this versatile, berry-intense cooler as a soup, an on-the-go shake – even a cereal topper. Tofu adds not only creaminess, but staying power; you'll feel sated a long time. If you serve it as a soup, garnish with mint to dramatize the color.

1 (12.3-ounce) package light and firm silken tofu

1 pound fresh or frozen strawberries, raspberries or blueberries

½ cup frozen apple juice concentrate

¼ cup nonfat yogurt

1 tablespoon honey (optional)

Pre-prep: Rinse and hull fresh berries, or partially thaw frozen berries.

1. Puree the tofu and berries in a blender or food processor; add apple juice concentrate, yogurt, and honey, if using, and process until blended, 1 to 2 minutes.

2. Serve immediately, or transfer to storage container, cover and chill.

Serves 4

Each 1 cup serving has approximately:

Cals: 143	*Sodium: 106 mg*	*Calcium: 93 mg*
Total fat: 1.3 g	*Chol: None*	*Carbs: 27 g*
Sat fat: 0.2 g	*Fiber: 2.5 g*	*Protein: 8 g*

pizza, pasta & pickups

pizza, pasta & pickups

Although Leek and Mushroom Manicotti tweaks a familiar dish, most of these recipes stretch our concept of pizza and pasta — and even burgers. Take Ancho Chile Pasta, redolent with chiles and garlic. Transformed with chewy corn pasta, chicken sausage, cilantro and corn, it's what Chili Mac would like to be when it grows up. Creamy Lemon Orzo will win over the most adamant tofu-phobic: Lemony-caper tang radiates through the silken tofu base, amplifying flavors in a surprising way. And you could put Turkey-Watercress Burgers in front of a dozen food critics, and none could identify the quirky melange of ingredients that produces such a wonderful, moist and meaty rush of flavors. Be brave: Experience the unexpected.

spanakopita pizza

The crust of this dazzling red, white and green pizza is golden, flaky phyllo pastry. A hit for brunch, lunch or summer supper, it's too loaded to lift like regular pizza. So put out plenty of knives and forks.

Olive oil cooking spray

3 cloves garlic, minced

1 large onion, finely chopped

3 (10-ounce) packages frozen spinach, thawed and squeezed dry

¼ cup chopped fresh basil

¼ cup chopped fresh parsley

1 tablespoon dried dill

¼ teaspoon nutmeg

2 teaspoons fresh lemon juice

8 sheets of phyllo dough, at room temperature

3 ounces feta cheese, crumbled

¼ cup Dijon mustard or horseradish mustard

3 ounces part-skim mozzarella cheese, grated

4 medium tomatoes, sliced

Pre-prep: Thaw spinach and squeeze dry. Bring phyllo to room temperature. Mince garlic; chop onion, basil and parsley; juice lemon; slice tomatoes.

1. Spray a large skillet with cooking spray, and sauté garlic and onions over medium heat for about 5 minutes.

2. Add spinach and sauté until all moisture has evaporated. Remove from heat and add basil, parsley, dill, nutmeg and lemon juice; mix well, set aside to cool.

3. Preheat oven to 400° F. Coat a 12x16-inch baking or pizza pan with cooking spray. Layer with phyllo sheets to cover pan, lightly spraying after each sheet with cooking spray. Finish by spraying the top of the final sheet and roll edges under. Bake 4 to 5 minutes; allow to cool.

4. Mix feta cheese into spinach mixture. After crust has cooled, carefully brush it with a thin coat of mustard. Don't worry if some flakes off; this won't show. Carefully spread spinach mixture on top. Add half the mozzarella. Arrange tomatoes side by side on top of spinach and cheese. Sprinkle with remaining mozzarella. Bake 20 to 25 minutes until cheese is melted and crust is golden.

Serves 6

Each serving has approximately:

Cals: 230	*Sodium: 522 mg*	*Calcium: 382 mg*
Total fat: 8.2 g	*Chol: 21 mg*	*Carbs: 29 g*
Sat fat: 3.9 g	*Fiber: 5 g*	*Protein: 13 g*

pizza, pasta & pickups

pizza, pasta & pickups

creamy lemon orzo

If you are tofu-phobic, get over it with this velvety sauce. Above and beyond its health benefits, blended tofu makes a fabulous sauce base.

1 (12.3-ounce) package light and firm silken tofu

½ cup water

3 green onions, minced

1 carrot, finely shredded

¼ cup fresh parsley or mint leaves, minced (divided use)

2 tablespoons capers, drained and minced

Grated peel of 1 lemon

2 to 3 tablespoons lemon juice

Freshly ground black pepper

1 (6-ounce) can solid white tuna, water packed, rinsed and well drained (optional, see note)

4 cups cooked orzo pasta or brown rice, rinsed (about 12 ounces uncooked, see note)

1 teaspoon salt or to taste

Pre-prep: Cook pasta or rice. Mince onions, parsley and capers; shred carrot; grate lemon peel; juice lemon (or lemons); drain and rinse tuna, if using.

1. Place tofu and water in blender or food processor bowl; blend until smooth and creamy. Transfer blended tofu to a large skillet or saucepan and add onions, carrot, half the parsley, capers, lemon peel, lemon juice and black pepper.

2. Bring to a boil over medium heat. Reduce heat, stir in tuna, if using, and pasta or rice; heat through. Garnish with remaining parsley or mint.

Serves 6

Each serving has approximately:

Cals: 238	*Sodium: 548 mg*	*Calcium: 42 mg*
Total fat: 1.5 g	*Chol: None*	*Carbs: 45 g*
Sat fat: 0.3 g	*Fiber: 2 g*	*Protein: 11 g*

note

Why canned tuna instead of fresh? Surprisingly, it is exquisite in this dish. Plus, it's an authentic ingredient in Mediterranean cuisine.

And why rinse the pasta or rice? The sauce has a nicer sheen and will be less apt to "clump" when you reheat it.

ancho chile pasta

Dappled with yellow, rust and green, this mildly spicy dish echoes the colors and flavors of the Southwest. Corn pasta adds a nubby, chewy texture.

2 cups water

2 dried ancho chiles

3 large cloves garlic

1 teaspoon dried oregano, crumbled

12 ounces uncooked pasta, preferably corn or whole wheat

Nonstick cooking spray

1 cup red bell pepper, cut in ¼-inch dice

2 tablespoons lime juice

1 tablespoon olive oil

6 ounces chicken or turkey sausage

1 cup frozen corn kernels, thawed

1 cup cilantro, minced (divided use)

½ teaspoon salt or to taste

1 cup nonfat yogurt (optional)

Pre-prep: Dice bell pepper; juice lime; remove sausage from casing; thaw corn; mince cilantro.

1. In a small pan, heat water to boiling, add dried chiles (see note) and simmer 5 minutes. Remove chiles, reserving cooking liquid. Remove stems and seeds from chiles and place in a blender or small processor bowl with the garlic and oregano. Process, gradually adding enough cooking liquid to make a smooth paste.

2. Bring a pot of salted water to a boil. Cook pasta until just al dente. Drain, reserving about ½ cup cooking water, keep pasta warm.

3. Meanwhile, coat a skillet with nonstick cooking spray and place over medium heat; sauté bell pepper until soft. Remove from heat, stir in pureed chile paste, lime juice and olive oil; set aside.

4. Crumble and cook sausage with low heat in microwave or in a small skillet; drain and add to pasta, along with corn, ¾ cup cilantro and salt to taste.

5. Stir about ½ cup hot pasta water into chile-paste mixture, until smooth; add to pasta mixture and toss. Mix remaining cilantro with yogurt and serve on the side, if desired.

Serves 6

Each serving has approximately:

Cals: 333	*Sodium: 515 mg*	*Calcium: 58 mg*
Total fat: 6.4 g	*Chol: 18 mg*	*Carbs: 57 g*
Sat fat: 1.1 g	*Fiber: 5 g*	*Protein: 15 g*

note

Some ancho chile peppers remain tough after cooking so you may want to cook one or two extra. But use only two.

pizza, pasta & pickups

jalapeño-pumpkin seed quesadillas

With pumpkin seeds instead of pine nuts, cilantro and parsley instead of basil, the spread for these quesadillas is like a pesto pico. Roasted Red Pepper Cream makes a smooth counterpart.

⅓ cup raw, unsalted pumpkin seeds

1 jalapeño pepper, seeded

3 large cloves garlic

1½ cups fresh cilantro, packed, rinsed and spun dry

1½ cups fresh parsley leaves, packed (preferably flat-leaf), rinsed and spun dry

1 teaspoon salt

1 tablespoon olive oil

8 whole-wheat soft flour tortillas

1 cup grated low-fat or nonfat Cheddar cheese

1 pound grilled chicken, shredded (optional)

Nonstick cooking spray

Roasted Red Pepper Cream (recipe at right)

Pre-prep: Make Roasted Red Pepper Cream. Seed jalapeño; wash and dry cilantro and parsley, remove large stems; grate cheese; shred chicken, if using.

1. Toast pumpkin seeds in a dry skillet over medium-high heat until they pop and jump; remove from heat. In a food processor, finely mince jalapeño and garlic. Add toasted pumpkin seeds, cilantro, parsley, salt and olive oil; blend until it reaches the consistency of paste.

2. Spread ¼ of the paste on a tortilla. Sprinkle with ¼ of the cheese and ¼ of the chicken, if using. Cover with another tortilla. Repeat, using remaining tortillas and fillings.

3. Spray a griddle or heavy skillet with cooking spray and place over medium-high heat. Add a quesadilla. When one side is toasted, about 2 minutes, spray top tortilla with cooking spray and turn. Continue to cook until the second side is toasted and cheese melts. Repeat with remaining quesadillas. Cut in halves or quarters. Serve with Roasted Red Pepper Cream.

Serves 4

Each serving has approximately:

Cals: 365	*Sodium: 886 mg*	*Calcium: 255 mg*
Total fat: 13.7 g	*Chol: 10 mg*	*Carbs: 45 g*
Sat fat: 3.4 g	*Fiber: 3 g*	*Protein: 17 g*

roasted red pepper cream

1 red bell pepper

1 cup light and firm silken tofu

1 tablespoon lemon juice

½ teaspoon salt or to taste

Black pepper to taste

1. Preheat oven to 400° F. Roast pepper for 20 to 25 minutes. Remove and let cool. Peel under running water.

2. Cut in half and discard stem, seeds and membrane. Cut in 3 to 4 pieces.

3. Blend all ingredients together in a food processor or blender.

variation

Instead of Red Pepper Cream, go green with ¼ cup basil pesto stirred into 2 cups yogurt.

southwest harvest pizza

B arbecue sauce adds subtle sweetness to this meal on a crust, but the heart of its flavors comes from the tangy marinade. If you can't bring yourself to burden a pizza crust with so many vegetables, the topping is also great over rice.

lime marinade

1 teaspoon olive oil

3 tablespoons lime juice

1 tablespoon minced garlic (4 to 5 cloves)

2 teaspoons ground cumin

2 teaspoons oregano

2 dried chipotle chiles, seeds removed, finely ground or 1 teaspoon chili powder

1 jalapeño pepper, seeded and finely minced

½ teaspoon salt or to taste

Mix all ingredients together.

8 ounces boneless, skinless chicken breast, cut in ½-inch cubes

Lime Marinade (recipe at left)

Nonstick cooking spray

½ red bell pepper, cut in ½-inch cubes

½ poblano pepper, cut in ½-inch cubes

1 cup julienned red onion

2 cups yellow squash, zucchini or a mix, cut in ½-inch cubes

1 (12-ounce) prepared pizza crust

¾ cup barbecue sauce

¼ cup chopped cilantro

½ cup corn, fresh roasted (see Page 17) or frozen, thawed

½ cup black beans, rinsed and drained (optional)

4 green onions, sliced

½ cup low-fat shredded Cheddar cheese

Pre-prep: Make marinade; cube chicken and place in a non-reactive bowl with marinade for at least 30 minutes. Roast corn or thaw. Cube peppers and squash; julienne onion; chop cilantro; rinse and drain beans, if using; slice green onions.

1. Preheat oven to 450º F. Drain chicken, reserving marinade. Coat wok or large skillet with cooking spray and place over medium-high heat. Add chicken and cook, stirring frequently. When nearly done (chicken will still feel soft, not firm), remove to a large bowl.

2. Add the peppers, onion and squash to the wok, stirring to quickly cook. If mixture sticks or fails to cook quickly, add some reserved marinade and cover for 1 or 2 minutes. When vegetables are nearly done, add them to the chicken. (May be prepared to this point and refrigerated.)

3. Place pizza crust on a large, sturdy baking sheet. Mix barbecue sauce and cilantro in a small bowl; spread on pizza crust. Evenly cover the sauce with the chicken and vegetables, then corn and black beans, if using. Sprinkle with green onions and cheese. Bake for 10 to 12 minutes, until crust is heated through and cheese is melted.

Serves 4

Each serving has approximately:

Cals: 554	*Sodium: 1,218 mg*	*Calcium: 211 mg*
Total fat: 9.1 g	*Chol: 44 mg*	*Carbs: 93 g*
Sat fat: 2.5 g	*Fiber: 7 g*	*Protein: 27 g*

pizza, pasta & pickups

oven roasted veggie pizza

Almost as quick as takeout, and so much fresher tasting, this pizza uses ready-made sauce and crust. Even diehard pepperoni fans will love this when you add the turkey sausage.

1 cup bottled marinara sauce

1 (12-inch) ready-made pizza crust

3 tablespoons minced basil

6 ounces turkey Italian sausage, crumbled and cooked (optional)

6 mushrooms, sliced

Oven Roasted Veggies, diced (see Page 106)

3 tablespoons shredded Parmesan or Romano cheese

Pre-prep: Make Oven Roasted Veggies and dice. Cook sausage, if using. Slice mushrooms; mince basil.

Preheat oven to 450° F. Spread marinara sauce on crust and sprinkle with basil. Mix sausage, if using, and mushrooms into diced vegetable mixture. Spread evenly over sauce; sprinkle with cheese and bake 15 to 20 minutes, until cheese is melted.

Serves 4

Each serving has approximately:

Cals: 346	*Sodium: 349 mg*	*Calcium: 125 mg*
Total fat: 8 g	*Chol: 5 mg*	*Carbs: 59 g*
Sat fat: 1.8 g	*Fiber: 6 g*	*Protein: 11 g*

variation

To make Oven Roasted Veggie Pasta, mix diced veggies with 1½ cups marinara sauce in a large saucepan over medium heat until heated through, about 5 minutes. Add 6 cups of cooked pasta to the sauce and gently toss to mix. Divide among 4 serving bowls; sprinkle with Parmesan and minced basil.

pizza, pasta & pickups

leek and mushroom manicotti

The sautéed vegetables give this filling lots of body, yet the egg roll wrappers keep it light.

1 (12.3-ounce) package light, firm tofu

1 cup nonfat ricotta cheese

6 tablespoons grated Parmesan cheese (divided use)

$\frac{1}{8}$ teaspoon nutmeg

$\frac{1}{4}$ cup fresh minced basil or 1 teaspoon dried

Olive oil cooking spray

8 ounces mushrooms, chopped (about 3 cups)

2 to 3 large leeks, white and light green part only, chopped (about 2 cups)

4 cloves garlic, minced

8 ready-made egg-roll wrappers

3 cups bottled marinara sauce plus some to pass at table, if desired

Pre-prep: Mince basil and garlic; chop mushrooms; trim root end and green leaves from leeks and rinse thoroughly, chop.

1. Preheat oven to 350° F. Crumble tofu into a small bowl. Add ricotta and 3 tablespoons Parmesan, nutmeg and basil; stir to blend well.

2. Spray a large skillet with cooking spray and place over medium-high heat. Add the mushrooms, leeks and garlic, and cover. After 3 to 4 minutes, remove the lid, lower heat and continue to cook, stirring often. When all moisture has evaporated and vegetables are tender, about 5 more minutes, allow to cool and combine with the ricotta mixture.

3. Spread about a third of the marinara sauce in the bottom of an 11x13-inch glass baking dish.

4. To assemble manicotti, place 2 heaping tablespoons of the cheese-vegetable filling on an egg-roll wrapper about 1 inch from the bottom and sides of the wrapper. Fold the bottom over to cover the filling, then fold in each side; finish by rolling like a burrito into a "packet"; place on top of sauce in baking dish. Repeat with remaining wrappers and filling, lining them up side by side, seam-side down.

5. Spray manicotti packets with cooking spray. Pour remaining marinara sauce over the manicotti, and sprinkle with the remaining Parmesan. Bake for 30 minutes, until cheese is melted. Pass additional sauce, if you like, as most of the sauce on the manicotti will be taken up in baking.

Serves 8

Each manicotti has approximately:

Cals: 201	*Sodium: 630 mg*	*Calcium: 268 mg*
Total fat: 2.9 g	*Chol: 8 mg*	*Carbs: 30 g*
Sat fat: 1 g	*Fiber: 1 g*	*Protein: 14 g*

variation

For a livelier sauce, sauté together 6 ounces turkey sausage, 1 red bell pepper (cut in strips) and 1 zucchini squash, cubed. Add 1 or 2 cups pasta sauce, heat and serve over the manicotti instead of plain bottled sauce.

pizza, pasta & pickups

mediterranean pasta sauce

So decadently rich and robust with olives and feta. Your taste buds can be tricked into sensing sausage flavor by adding ½ teaspoon crushed fennel seed.

Olive oil cooking spray

2 medium zucchini, cut into ³/₄-inch dice

1 medium onion, diced

4 cloves garlic, minced

1 (28-ounce) can crushed tomatoes

1 (15-ounce) can diced tomatoes

1 tablespoon dried oregano

¼ teaspoon freshly ground pepper

1 (2-ounce) can sliced ripe olives, drained and chopped

8 cups cooked pasta (16 ounces dried, corkscrew, penne or ruffle) or 1 cooked spaghetti squash

3 to 4 ounces feta, crumbled

¼ cup minced mint leaves or 1 tablespoon dried mint

¼ cup minced basil

Pre-prep: Dice zucchini and onion; mince garlic, mint and basil; chop olives.

1. Coat a large skillet with cooking spray and place over medium-high heat. Add zucchini, onion and garlic; sauté until zucchini is tender-crisp, about 5 minutes. Stir in tomatoes, oregano and pepper.

2. Bring to boil; reduce heat, cover and simmer 5 minutes. Stir in olives; cook 3 more minutes.

3. Toss cooked pasta with sauce and add feta. Just before serving, sprinkle with mint and basil.

Serves 6

Each serving has approximately:

Cals: 301	*Sodium: 819 mg*	*Calcium: 167 mg*
Total fat: 6.5 g	*Chol: 15 mg*	*Carbs: 50 g*
Sat fat: 0.2 g	*Fiber: 4 g*	*Protein: 11 g*

tip

Mint condition: If you have an abundance of fresh mint, here's a way to dry and store it. Pull the leaves off, place them in a single layer between two paper towels and heat them in the microwave on High (100% power). Check after 1 minute; they should be dark and shriveled. If they still seem a little moist, nuke for 30 seconds more. Let them continue to air-dry a few hours before storing in an airtight container in the pantry for up to six months.

smoked turkey–cranberry chutney roll-ups

You can easily substitute Thanksgiving leftovers, even pork tenderloin or chicken, for the smoked turkey in this beautiful wrapper.

1½ tablespoons minced fresh ginger

1 (12-ounce) bag cranberries

¾ cup sugar

1 cup orange marmalade

½ cup walnuts, toasted and finely chopped (see Page 17)

1½ teaspoons Chinese 5-spice powder

¼ teaspoon cloves

8 ounces reduced-fat cream cheese, room temperature

8 ounces nonfat cream cheese, room temperature

1 pound thinly sliced smoked turkey (see note)

16 whole wheat tortillas

Spinach or leaf lettuce

Pre-prep: Toast and chop walnuts; bring cream cheese to room temperature. Mince ginger.

1. Preheat oven to 350° F. Combine ginger, cranberries and sugar in 13x9½-inch baking pan, tightly cover with aluminum foil and bake for 50 minutes. Remove from oven; add orange marmalade, walnuts and spices, stir well and cool to room temperature.

2. Meanwhile, whip cream cheeses together in a food processor until smooth.

3. Spread each tortilla with a thin layer of cream cheese; leave a 1-inch perimeter around the edges. Cover with a layer of the cranberries, followed by a layer of sliced turkey; top with spinach or lettuce leaves.

4. Tightly tuck one side of wrapper, keeping spinach flat; roll away from you, jellyroll style. With the seam side down, cut with sharp knife into 1-inch slices for appetizers or in half for larger servings. Serve with cut end exposed to show the red, white and green.

Serves 16

Each wrap has approximately:

Cals: 257	Sodium: 598 mg	Calcium: 100 mg
Total fat: 5.1 g	Chol: 17 mg	Carbs: 41 g
Sat fat: 1.8 g	Fiber: 11 g	Protein: 11 g

note

If you use meats that are chunky rather than sliced thin, the wrapper will look more like a burrito.

turkey–watercress burgers

Messy to make, these burgers are surprisingly juicy, delicious and satisfying — and hold together perfectly on the grill. Alternatively, use the meat mixture as a filling for succulent stuffed peppers.

8 ounces ground turkey breast

1½ cups finely chopped watercress, arugula or spinach

1½ cups finely chopped mushrooms

1 egg white

3 tablespoons Parmesan cheese

¾ teaspoon freshly ground black pepper

½ teaspoon salt or to taste

Olive oil cooking spray

4 Italian hard rolls, split

Pre-prep: Chop watercress and mushrooms. Separate egg, discard yolk. Preheat broiler or grill.

1. Mix together all ingredients except cooking spray and rolls in a bowl and shape into 4 (1-inch thick) patties. Don't worry if some greens and mushrooms stick to your fingers or to the bowl.

2. Coat broiler pan or grill with cooking spray. Cook patties 3 minutes, spray patties with cooking spray, turn and cook until done, about 4 more minutes. Heat rolls over grill or in oven 2 minutes, if desired. Serve burgers with coarse-ground mustard and slices of orange or tomato.

Serves 4

Each burger has approximately:

Cals:314	*Sodium: 795 mg*	*Calcium: 143 mg*
Total fat: 4.7 g	*Chol: 50 mg*	*Carbs: 39 g*
Sat fat: 1.3 g	*Fiber: 0.5 g*	*Protein: 27 g*

main dish
salads

main dish salads

Anchored on a base of interesting greens, the most memorable main dish salads satisfy deeply with point-counterpoint textures and flavors. Forget those limp salads that leave us restive, prowling the kitchen two hours later for something to fill the void. Almost all the main dish salads here include meat, although it doesn't dominate the plate. (One could easily mix and match around it for vegetarian.) Minted chicken — quick-sautéed strips marinated with garlic, jalapeño and mint — goes on top of raspberry dressing-tossed greens with cinnamon-spiked Fruited Couscous and a riot of fresh fruit. Chicken roulade stuffed with goat cheese and spinach crowns a bed of fabulous quick-sautéed apples, mushrooms and assertive greens, such as arugula, Swiss chard or escarole. Creole Seafood Salad matches elegant crabmeat with garlicky roasted new potatoes, capers and mushrooms atop intense Creole-dressed greens. If the recipes seem long or complicated, remember: You're replacing an entire meal — meat, potatoes and vegetable — with one salad. We just remembered: These salads might not fill you all the way up; there still might be just enough room for bread and dessert.

minted chicken with raspberry dressing and fruited couscous

Spicy minted chicken provides cool counterpoint to raspberry-dressed greens, sweet fruit and mellow Fruited Couscous.

12 ounces boneless, skinless chicken breast, cut into 1x3-inch strips

2 cloves garlic, minced

1 jalapeño pepper, red if possible, minced

1 teaspoon canola oil

1 tablespoon vermouth or white wine

1 bunch of fresh mint leaves, minced, but reserve 4 sprigs for garnish

Olive oil cooking spray

8 cups mixed salad greens

Raspberry Dressing (see Page 80)

2 cups fresh fruit, cut in bite-size pieces (any combination such as grapes, blueberries, strawberries, nectarines, papaya, kiwi or mango)

1⅓ cups Fruited Couscous (see Page 120)

Pre-prep: Make Raspberry Dressing and Fruited Couscous. Cut chicken into strips. Mince garlic, jalapeño and mint; rinse, dry and tear greens. Prepare fruit.

1. Combine chicken with garlic, jalapeño, oil, vermouth and mint and allow to marinate, refrigerated, for at least 1 hour.

2. Coat skillet with cooking spray and place over medium heat. Add chicken pieces and quickly cook, turning frequently. Remove from heat.

3. Toss greens with dressing; divide among 4 large plates. Arrange mixed fruit pieces and ⅓ cup of couscous on top of greens. Add cooked chicken and garnish with mint sprigs.

Serves 4

Each serving has approximately:

Cals: 409	*Sodium: 652 mg*	*Calcium: 122 mg*
Total fat: 7.7 g	*Chol: 52 g*	*Carbs: 63 g*
Sat fat: 1 g	*Fiber: 8 g*	*Protein: 25 g*

main dish salads

asian noodles on sesame-spinach salad

The secret of success with this wonderful salad duo is to make the asian noodles ahead of time. We've left the dishes as distinct recipes because each stands so beautifully on its own.

2 cups snow peas, halved lengthwise

8 ounces soba (buckwheat) or udon (wheat) noodles

1 large red bell pepper, cut in thin strips, about 2x¼ inches

1 medium carrot, grated

Spicy Tahini-Ginger Dressing (recipe at right)

Sesame-Spinach Salad (recipe on next page)

Pre-prep: Make Spicy Tahini-Ginger Dressing. Cut snow peas and bell peppers; grate carrot.

1. Drop snow peas into a pot of boiling water; when water returns to a boil, cook snow peas 1 to 2 minutes. Lift the snow peas out with a slotted spoon and quickly plunge into ice water; drain well and set aside. Meanwhile, keep the water boiling for the noodles.

2. Break noodles in half; add to boiling water. When water returns to a boil, cook 5 minutes, or just until al dente. Drain and rinse with cool water.

3. Combine cooked noodles, snow peas, red pepper and carrot in a large serving bowl; add the dressing and stir gently. (This can be done 1 to 2 days in advance; refrigerate until ready to use). Chill at least 30 minutes.

4. Prepare Sesame-Spinach Salad. At serving time, divide spinach salad among 4 plates. Top with Asian noodle salad. Add garnishes.

Serves 4

Each serving (noodle salad only) has approximately:

Cals: 303	*Sodium: 503 mg*	*Calcium: 45 mg*
Total fat: 3.7 g	*Chol: None*	*Carbs: 59 g*
Sat fat: < 1 g	*Fiber: 7 g*	*Protein: 9 g*

spicy tahini ginger dressing

1 tablespoon sesame tahini paste

⅓ cup water

3 tablespoons rice vinegar

3 tablespoons reduced-sodium soy sauce

2 tablespoons grated fresh ginger

3 cloves garlic

1 tablespoon honey

1 teaspoon Asian chile sauce

Salt to taste

Place all ingredients in a blender or small food processor and blend until smooth.

sesame-spinach salad

1 tablespoon plus 2 teaspoons toasted sesame seeds (divided use, see Page 17)

⅓ cup rice vinegar

2 teaspoons honey

2 teaspoons reduced-sodium soy sauce

½ teaspoon toasted sesame oil

Dash cayenne pepper

8 cups spinach, or mixed greens, torn into bite-size pieces

1 to 2 medium cucumbers, peeled and thinly sliced

2 to 3 medium tomatoes, cut into wedges

⅓ cup green onions, sliced, for garnish

2 tablespoons minced mint leaves

Pre-prep: Toast sesame seeds; rinse, dry and tear spinach; peel and slice cucumbers; cut tomatoes; slice onions; mince mint.

1. To make the dressing, mix 1 tablespoon sesame seeds, vinegar, honey, soy sauce, sesame oil and cayenne in a small bowl.

2. In a large bowl, toss salad greens, cucumbers and tomatoes with dressing. Garnish with green onions, remaining sesame seeds and mint. (Note: When combining this salad with the Asian noodle salad, reserve garnish until after both have been plated.)

Serves 4

Each serving has approximately:

Cals: 176   *Sodium: 718 mg*   *Calcium: 159 mg*
Total fat: 4 g *Chol: None*   *Carbs: 30 g*
Sat fat: 0.5 g *Fiber: 6 g*   *Protein: 7 g*

main dish salads

cajun chicken salad with summer fruits

Spicy pan-seared chicken, roast new potatoes and sweet summer fruits in Sesame Dressing are dazzling over red and green leaf lettuce.

1 pound boneless, skinless chicken breast halves

Cajun or blackening seasoning

Olive oil cooking spray

8 cups mixed red and green leaf lettuce, torn into bite-size pieces

3 medium nectarines or plums, sliced

1 cup red grapes

3 kiwis, peeled, cut in half and thinly sliced

12 small roasted red new potatoes, quartered (see Page 108)

Sesame Dressing (recipe at right)

1 mango, sliced

Pre-prep: Roast potatoes. Make Sesame Dressing. Rinse, dry and tear lettuce; slice nectarines; peel kiwi and mango and slice.

1. Flatten each chicken breast to uniform thickness by placing it between 2 sheets of wax paper and pounding with the flat side of a meat mallet.

2. Generously coat each side of chicken with seasoning; then lightly coat with cooking spray.

3. Heat a seasoned cast-iron skillet over high heat until the skillet begins to smoke. Add chicken in a single layer and cook for 2 minutes; turn and cook 2 more minutes. Remove and cool slightly or refrigerate to use later. Cut chicken into ½x2-inch slices.

4. In a large salad bowl, mix greens, nectarines, grapes, kiwi, potatoes and chicken. Toss gently with the dressing. Divide salad among 4 serving plates and arrange mango slices on top.

Serves 4

Each serving has approximately:

Cals: 491	*Sodium: 989 mg*	*Calcium: 141 mg*
Total fat: 7.5 g	*Chol: 69 mg*	*Carbs: 76 g*
Sat fat: 1.3 g	*Fiber: 9 g*	*Protein: 32 g*

sesame dressing

2 teaspoons sesame seeds

½ cup balsamic vinegar

¼ cup red wine vinegar

¼ cup reduced-sodium soy sauce

1½ tablespoons honey

1 teaspoon Dijon mustard

2 teaspoons sesame oil

Dash cayenne pepper (optional)

1. Preheat oven to 400° F and toast sesame seeds in a small pan for about 6 minutes.

2. Combine with remaining ingredients and mix well.

main dish salads

seafood on creole greens

Creamy Creole Dressing adds remoulade sparks to lettuce, mushrooms, potatoes and seafood. There's a sensory K.O. in every bite.

8 cups mixed greens, such as romaine, red leaf lettuce and radicchio, rinsed and torn into bite-size pieces

1 to 2 cucumbers, peeled and sliced

1 red onion, julienned

Creole Dressing (recipe at left)

2 tablespoons capers

8 fresh mushrooms, sliced

12 small new potatoes roasted with garlic cloves, or sweet potato chunks (see Page 108)

1 pound shrimp, boiled, peeled and deveined (see note) or crabmeat

½ avocado, sliced (optional)

4 tomatoes, quartered

12 Nicoise or Kalamata olives

Pre-prep: Prepare and cook shrimp, if using. Roast potatoes. Make dressing. Wash, dry and tear salad greens; slice cucumbers, mushrooms and avocado, if using; julienne onion; quarter tomatoes.

1. In a large salad bowl, combine lettuces, cucumber and onion. Toss with about ¾ of the dressing.

2. Divide salad among serving 4 plates and arrange capers, mushrooms, potatoes and shrimp or crabmeat on top. Garnish with optional avocado, if desired, tomatoes and olives; drizzle remaining dressing over each plate.

Serves 4

Each serving has approximately:

Cals: 330	*Sodium: 832 mg*	*Calcium: 174 mg*
Total fat: 7.9 g	*Chol: 223 mg*	*Carbs: 35 g*
Sat fat: 1.3 g	*Fiber: 7 g*	*Protein: 30 g*

creole dressing

2 cloves garlic

1 tablespoon lemon juice

2 tablespoons Creole mustard

4 teaspoons Dijon mustard

1 tablespoon horseradish

2 teaspoons canola oil

¼ cup cream sherry

1 teaspoon brown sugar

¼ teaspoon salt

Freshly ground black pepper

1. Finely mince garlic and place in a small bowl.

2. Add remaining ingredients and mix thoroughly.

note

Grilled or Cajun Chicken (see opposite page) can be substituted for seafood. Roasted corn kernels can also be added.

main dish salads

vietnamese noodle salad with broccoli and peanuts

Like soy sauce, Asian fish sauce is high in sodium. But to omit this important Thai-Vietnamese ingredient is to miss out on an extraordinary flavor experience. Unless you're salt sensitive, let it slide.

6 ounces dried Asian rice noodles (or rice sticks)

1 to 1¼ pounds broccoli, cut into florets

½ cup water

4 to 5 cloves garlic, finely minced

½ cup Asian fish sauce

½ cup fresh lime juice

2½ tablespoons sugar

¾ teaspoon dried hot pepper flakes

4 tablespoons unsalted peanuts, coarsely chopped (divided use)

½ cup mixed fresh mint, basil and cilantro, finely minced (divided use)

8 cups mixed leaf lettuce and spinach, rinsed and torn into bite-size pieces

3 to 4 medium tomatoes, cubed

Pre-prep: Cut broccoli into florets; mince garlic and herbs; juice lime; chop peanuts; rinse, dry and tear greens; cube tomatoes.

1. Bring a large pot of water to rapid boil and cook noodles for 5 minutes; remove with a slotted spoon and drain, but keep water boiling. Rinse noodles in cold water, drain again; set aside. Add broccoli to boiling water and blanch for 2 to 3 minutes; plunge into ice water; drain and set aside.

2. In a small jar, mix water, garlic, fish sauce, lime juice, sugar, pepper flakes, 1 tablespoon peanuts and about half of the fresh herbs; shake to mix. Or, mix ingredients in a small bowl. Pour about half the dressing over the noodles and mix well.

3. Toss greens, tomatoes and broccoli with remaining dressing; divide among 4 serving plates. Place noodles on top of the greens and tomatoes. If any dressing remains in the bottom of either mixing bowl, pour it over salads, if desired. Garnish with remaining herbs and peanuts.

Serves 4

Each serving has approximately:

Cals: 358   *Sodium: 1,967 mg*   *Calcium: 293 mg*
Total fat: 6 g   *Chol: None*   *Carbs: 67 g*
Sat fat: 0.8 g   *Fiber: 8 g*   *Protein: 15 g*

grilled tuna on salad with rosemary dressing

A little fire in the dressing fires up the flavors of mustard-grilled tuna and rosemary-spiked greens. Feta adds creamy richness.

4 (1-inch thick) fresh yellowfin tuna steaks, about 1 pound

Grilling Paste (see note)

Olive oil cooking spray

8 cups mixed greens, rinsed and torn into bite-size pieces

Rosemary Dressing (recipe at left)

1½ cups cooked green beans (optional)

1 medium red onion, julienned

2 tomatoes, diced

1 red bell pepper, julienned

12 small roasted potatoes (optional, see Page 108)

1 medium cucumber, peeled, seeded and sliced

2 ounces feta cheese, crumbled

Pre-prep: Make dressing and grilling paste. Cook green beans and potatoes, if using. Rinse, dry and tear greens; julienne onion and pepper; dice tomatoes; peel and slice cucumber.

1. Preheat oven or outdoor grill to 500° F or prepare a grill with hot coals. Coat both sides of fish with grilling paste and spray with olive oil cooking spray.

2. Heat a well-seasoned cast-iron skillet to the point of smoking on the grill (15 to 20 minutes) or on a well-vented kitchen stove.

3. To prepare tuna on the stove, spray hot pan with cooking spray just before adding fish. Sear the tuna for 2 minutes on one side over high heat; turn and place in the oven for 4 to 5 minutes. If using an outdoor grill, spray hot pan with cooking spray just before adding fish. Cook 3 to 4 minutes, turn with a spatula; cook 3 to 4 minutes on the second side. (Don't worry if some of the mustard coating sticks to the skillet.) Tuna is done when it feels firm to the touch; it should still be pink in the middle, like a medium steak. Allow fish to cool.

4. While fish is cooling, toss salad greens with ³/₄ of the dressing and arrange greens on 4 large plates. Slice tuna about ¼-inch thick and arrange on top of greens along with green beans, if using, onion, tomatoes, red pepper, roasted potatoes, if using, and cucumbers. Top with feta, and drizzle with remaining dressing.

Serves 4

Each serving has approximately:

Cals: 307	*Sodium: 328 mg*	*Calcium: 188 mg*
Total fat: 11 g	*Chol: 63 mg*	*Carbs: 18*
Sat fat: 3.3 g	*Fiber: 4.7 g*	*Protein: 32 g*

rosemary dressing

1 teaspoon anchovy paste

2 tablespoons sherry wine vinegar

2 tablespoons lime juice

¼ cup cream sherry

2 tablespoons brown sugar

2 teaspoons dried oregano

1 teaspoon dried rosemary

4 teaspoons olive oil with hot chile peppers (see note)

Salt to taste

Whisk all ingredients together in a small bowl.

note

If you can't find olive oil with chile peppers, use extra-virgin olive oil and ¹/₄ teaspoon of crushed red pepper. For the grilling paste, mix 3 tablespoons Dijon mustard with 2 tablespoons any combination of chopped basil, rosemary, tarragon, green peppercorns and/or capers.

main dish salads

hearty mediterranean salad with basil vinaigrette

If you secretly doubt that a salad can be an entire meal, try this one to become a believer. To save prep time, make the bulgur salad ahead and buy some roasted chicken.

12 ounces fresh asparagus spears or 2 cups sugar snap peas

10 cups mixed salad greens and radicchio, torn into bite-size pieces

Basil Vinaigrette (recipe at right)

12 ounces cooked chicken, turkey, pork tenderloin or seafood, cut in bite-size pieces

1 cup julienned purple onion

2½ cups papaya, peeled and cut in ¼x3-inch slices

3 cups Bulgur Salad With Sun-Dried Tomatoes, Basil and Almonds (see Page 111)

2 tablespoons minced fresh basil

2 tablespoons chopped, toasted almonds (optional)

Pre-prep: Make vinaigrette and bulgur salad. Cook meat, cut into pieces. Clean and prep asparagus or sugar snaps; slice onions and papaya; mince basil; chop and toast almonds, if using (see Page 17).

1. Place asparagus or sugar snaps in a glass dish with a small amount of water and cover. Microwave on High (100% power) about 3 minutes and plunge quickly into ice water to stop cooking. Drain and set aside.

2. Place salad greens in a large salad bowl and toss with ¾ of the vinaigrette. Divide among 4 large dinner plates.

3. Add the chicken, onion, papaya and asparagus or sugar snaps to the salad bowl and gently toss with remaining vinaigrette.

4. Arrange chicken, onion and papaya evenly atop the greens. Place several asparagus spears together, tips pointing toward outside the plate. Or, arrange sugar snaps.

5. For each plate, fill a ¾-cup measuring cup or ramekin with bulgur salad and invert over the salad greens close to the stem ends of the asparagus; tap on the bottom to unmold.

6. Garnish with basil and toasted almonds, if desired.

basil vinaigrette

2 tablespoons minced fresh basil, or 1 teaspoon dried basil and ½ teaspoon dried rosemary

¼ cup balsamic vinegar

2 cloves garlic, minced

1 shallot, finely minced

½ teaspoon anchovy paste

1 tablespoon basil-flavored olive oil or extra-virgin olive oil

3 tablespoons frozen apple juice concentrate

½ teaspoon salt, or to taste

Freshly ground pepper to taste

Combine ingredients; mix well.

Serves 4

Each serving has approximately:

Cals: 306	*Sodium: 422 mg*	*Calcium: 112 mg*
Total fat: 7.5 g	*Chol: 72 mg*	*Carbs: 27 g*
Sat fat: 1.5 g	*Fiber: 7 g*	*Protein: 32 g*

main dishes

main dishes

Trying to impose plant-centered cuisine on a meat-centered culture is like trying to switch kids from MTV to the history channel: What's good for them isn't necessarily what they like. So we won't tell you how to fix your favorite steak and chops; you already know. But we will try to woo you with some delicious entrees beyond the red-meat orbit, many grilled to intensify their flavors. Honey-Ginger Glazed Chicken, which turns a beautiful mahogany brown, is as simple as grilling steak. Rosemary-Citrus Snapper and Peppers fills the kitchen with orange, lemon and rosemary aromas. And Gaucho Chicken is a culinary cheap thrill: Serrano chiles are lodged between bone and flesh, little fire bombs for the unsuspecting. Some of the recipes in this chapter do have a strong vegetable component, like Thai Veggie Omelet and Curried Shrimp with Basmati and Peas. But more than anything, this chapter acknowledges the way we eat and the way we like to eat—ripping flesh from bones. Without apology.

honey–ginger glazed chicken

This deceptively simple recipe is a knockout. A whole rotisserie-roasted chicken is best, but you can achieve similar results using chicken pieces – bone-in for best flavor. Side with Curried Carrots.

1 (3-pound) chicken, skin removed, or 4 (6- to 8-ounce) chicken breast halves, bone-in, skin removed

Honey-Ginger Marinade (recipe at left)
Olive oil cooking spray

1. Remove skin and all visible fat from chicken.

2. Place chicken in large covered container and coat with marinade; refrigerate 4 to 8 hours.

3. Soak wood chips in water 10 to 20 minutes. Heat grill until very hot. Drain chicken and discard marinade. If using whole chicken, secure legs and wings with string. When grill is ready, place wood chips on fire. Secure chicken on rotisserie over medium heat. Cook 1 hour to 1 hour 15 minutes. Chicken will become darker the last 10 minutes.

4. If using breasts, coat with cooking spray and place bone-side down about 8 minutes over medium-high heat; turn and continue to cook about 8 to 10 more minutes. Remove when meat is firm and coating is very dark brown.

Serves 4

Each serving has approximately:

Cals: 333
Total fat: 11.8 g
Sat fat: 3.2 g

Sodium: 283 mg
Chol: 150 mg
Fiber: < 1 g

Calcium: 32 mg
Carbs: 4 g
Protein: 50 g

honey ginger marinade

3 tablespoons grated ginger

4 cloves garlic, minced

1 teaspoon sesame oil

2 tablespoons reduced sodium soy sauce

2 tablespoons Worcestershire sauce

1 tablespoon honey

1 tablespoon red wine vinegar

Pre-prep:
Grate ginger; mince garlic.

Combine all ingredients and mix well.

main dishes

chicken roulade on sautéed greens

Tossing the greens in the same skillet used to cook the chicken yields a rich, deep flavor.

3 tablespoons (2 ounces) goat cheese

1 tablespoon minced fresh tarragon (divided use)

2 tablespoons minced fresh basil (divided use)

1 (10-ounce) package frozen spinach, thawed and squeezed dry

2 egg whites

Freshly ground black pepper

4 (5-ounce) boneless, skinless chicken breast halves

½ teaspoon salt or to taste

Olive oil cooking spray

1 tablespoon extra-virgin olive oil

1 cup apple slices, ⅛-inch thick

8 ounces mushrooms, sliced thick

2 tablespoons minced shallots

1 pound strong-flavored mixed greens such as arugula, escarole, baby mustard greens, Swiss chard or Napa cabbage

2 tablespoons balsamic vinegar

Pre-prep: Mince tarragon and basil; thaw and squeeze moisture from spinach; slice apples (do not peel) and mushrooms; mince shallots; rinse and dry greens, remove woody stems and tear into bite-size pieces.

1. Preheat oven to 450° F. In a small bowl, mix goat cheese, 2 teaspoons tarragon and 1 tablespoon basil, spinach, egg whites and pepper to taste until well blended. Set aside.

2. Place chicken breasts between 2 sheets of wax paper and pound with the flat side of a meat mallet until thin. Season with salt and pepper.

3. Place ¼ of the spinach mixture in the center of each breast. Start at one end and roll the chicken over the spinach. The spinach will peek out at each end; with your fingers, gently pack it toward the center.

4. Coat a large nonstick skillet with olive oil cooking spray and place over medium heat. When hot, add the rolled chicken breasts. Partially cover and cook for 3 to 4 minutes; turn and cook another 3 to 4 minutes until golden brown; remove to an oven-proof dish.

5. Roast chicken rolls in oven 5 minutes, then turn; bake until firm to the touch, about 5 minutes more. Remove from oven and keep warm.

6. Return skillet to medium-high heat and add olive oil. Sauté apple, mushrooms and shallots about 2 minutes, then add greens, tossing quickly with tongs; remove skillet from heat, drizzle with the vinegar, toss again. Season with salt and pepper and remaining herbs. Divide warm salad among 4 large plates and top each with a roulade.

Serves 4

Each serving has approximately:

Cals: 301	Sodium: 470 mg	Calcium: 191 mg
Total fat: 11 g	Chol: 92 mg	Carbs: 14 g
Sat fat: 3.7 g	Fiber: 3.5 g	Protein: 38 g

main dishes

chile-rubbed pan-fried chicken

Ugly and brown, what this chicken lacks in visual appeal it more than makes up for in sumptuous flavor. Serve with Hot Potatoes with Roasted Corn and Poblano Peppers and Mango-Cilantro Salsa.

4 tablespoons chili powder

2 tablespoons brown sugar

¼ cup fresh cilantro, minced

1 to 2 tablespoons water

2 teaspoons cumin seeds

½ cup cornmeal

¾ teaspoon salt or to taste

¾ teaspoon pepper

¼ teaspoon cayenne pepper

4 small boneless, skinless chicken breast halves (about 1½ pounds)

Olive oil cooking spray

Pre-prep: Finely mince cilantro.

1. In a small bowl, mix chili powder, brown sugar and cilantro; add just enough water to make a thick paste. Set aside.

2. In another small bowl, mix cumin seeds, cornmeal, salt, pepper and cayenne; place half the mixture on a large dinner plate. Reserve remaining cornmeal mixture.

3. Place chicken breasts between 2 sheets of wax paper and pound to about ⅜-inch thickness with a meat mallet.

4. Using a rubber spatula, coat 1 side of the flattened breasts with chili paste. Lay breasts, paste-side down, in the cornmeal mixture. Use the spatula to coat top of the chicken with chili paste. (You may not need all of it.) Sprinkle on and pat in as much of the remaining cornmeal mixture as needed to thoroughly coat the top of the chicken.

5. Coat a heavy nonstick skillet with cooking spray and place over medium heat. Add chicken and cook about 3 minutes. Before turning, spray the top sides with cooking spray. Turn and continue to cook about 3 more minutes; the chicken should be firm. Serve immediately or allow to cool to room temperature.

Serves 4

Each serving has approximately:

Calories: 319	*Chol: 104 mg*	*Calcium: 57 mg*
Total fat: 6.2 g	*Sodium: 609 mg*	*Carbs: 25 g*
Sat fat: 1.3 g	*Fiber: 4 g*	*Protein: 40 g*

tip

Happy greens: To prolong the shelf life of cilantro and parsley, place the stems in water in a jar or glass, as you would cut flowers. Cover with a plastic-bag "hood" and replace in the refrigerator. It creates its own little humidified container.

main dishes

cornish hens provençal

T he lavender flowers make this rustic dish so elegant. For a memorable meal, serve with Tomatoes Provençal and Mashed Potatoes With Turnips, Leeks and Horseradish.

3 (1½- to 2-pound) Cornish game hens or 4½ pounds chicken pieces, skin removed

1 cup dry white wine

¼ cup Cognac (optional)

1 tablespoon dried lavender flowers (see note)

1 teaspoon salt

1 tablespoon dried thyme

2 cloves garlic, minced

1 tablespoon celery seed

1 teaspoon white pepper

1 teaspoon Worcestershire sauce

1 teaspoon hot pepper sauce

1 tablespoon olive oil

Pre-prep: Mince garlic.

1. Using sharp kitchen scissors, cut game hens in half by removing the backbone of each: Start at the tail and cut along the backbone to the neck on each side. Remove the last joint of the wing, or tuck it underneath the wing.

2. Mix together wine, Cognac, if using, lavender, salt, thyme, garlic, celery seed, pepper, Worcestershire and pepper sauces and olive oil for marinade.

3. Arrange game hens or chicken meaty-side down in glass or plastic container and pour the marinade over them. Cover in refrigerator at least 6 hours or overnight.

4. Preheat oven to 425° F. Reserving the marinade, remove poultry and place meaty-side up on uncovered roasting rack. Roast for 25 minutes or until juices run clear when knife is inserted into the thigh. Remove poultry from oven and allow to stand, covered, for about 10 minutes before serving.

5. Place marinade in a skillet and boil over high heat until volume is reduced by half, about 10 minutes.

6. Serve half a bird per person; spoon reduced marinade over top.

Serves 6

Each serving (without skin) has approximately:

Cals: 470   *Sodium: 733 mg*   *Calcium: 55 mg*
Total fat: 16.8 g   *Chol: 200 mg*   *Carbs: 2 g*
Sat fat: 4.6 g   *Fiber: <1 g*   *Protein: 66 g*

note

Use untreated or organic lavender flowers, often in the potpourri section of natural food stores.

main dishes

fruited moroccan chicken

Serve this fragrant, sensuous melange of chicken, fruits and spices over wild rice, couscous or quinoa.

Olive oil cooking spray

1 tablespoon olive oil

4 skinless chicken breasts, bone-in (about 2 pounds)

1 teaspoon salt, or to taste, and freshly ground black pepper to taste

2 onions, chopped

½ teaspoon ground cinnamon

½ teaspoon ground ginger

½ teaspoon ground cumin

1 (14.5-ounce) can fat-free, reduced-sodium chicken broth

4 ounces kumquats, quartered lengthwise and seeded (see note)

4 ounces pitted prunes, diced

1½ tablespoons honey

1 pound butternut squash, peeled, seeded and cut into ¾-inch cubes

2 tablespoons minced fresh cilantro

Pre-prep: Chop onions; quarter and seed kumquats; dice prunes; cube squash; mince cilantro.

1. Preheat oven to 350° F. Coat a large, heavy, oven-proof skillet with cooking spray, add olive oil and place over medium-high heat. Sprinkle chicken with salt and pepper, place in skillet and brown, about 6 minutes per side. Transfer chicken to plate and keep warm; chicken needn't be done.

2. Add onions to skillet, reduce heat to medium and sauté until very tender and beginning to brown, about 8 minutes. Add cinnamon, ginger and cumin, and stir until fragrant, about 30 seconds.

3. Add chicken broth, increase heat and bring to boil, scraping up browned bits from bottom of the skillet. Stir in kumquats, prunes, honey and squash. Lay chicken, flesh-side down, on top of fruit and liquid.

4. Cover skillet and place in oven. Braise until chicken is cooked through, about 25 minutes; remove chicken to covered container to keep warm.

5. Uncover skillet, return to oven until liquid thickens to sauce consistency, about 15 minutes. Season to taste with salt and pepper. (You can make this a day ahead, cover and refrigerate. Warm, covered, over medium heat.) Garnish with cilantro.

Serves 4

Each serving has approximately:

Cals: 399	Sodium: 743 mg	Calcium: 119 mg
Total fat: 7.6 g	Chol: 92 mg	Carbs: 46 g
Sat fat: 1.6 g	Fiber: 4 g	Protein: 39 g

note

If kumquats are not available, substitute tangerines or thin-skinned oranges. Dice whole fruit, peel and all, into ½-inch pieces; remove seeds and any large pieces of membrane.

main dishes

gaucho chicken
spiked with peppers

O K, so this has nothing to do with real gauchos – except that they would probably love its tongue-searing bite.

Olive oil cooking spray

6 serrano chiles, cut in half (seeded, if desired)

4 skinless chicken breast halves, bone-in (about 2 pounds)

Kitchen Bouquet

$^1/_2$ teaspoon salt, or to taste, and freshly ground black pepper to taste

Pre-prep: Cut chiles in half and remove seeds, if desired.

1. Spray skillet with cooking spray and place over high heat; add serrano chiles. Cook, turning twice, until well browned, about 5 minutes; remove from skillet and allow to cool.

2. Using a sharp paring knife, poke a hole along the bone of a chicken breast and push in a chile half. Continue around each breast, using 3 serrano halves per chicken breast.

3. Brush Kitchen Bouquet on both sides of breasts; season with salt and pepper; spray both sides with cooking spray.

4. Prepare outdoor grill. Coat grate with cooking spray; place chicken, bone-side down over medium-high heat. After 8 minutes, turn; check after 8 more minutes. Chicken will be firm to the touch when done.

Serves 4

Each serving has approximately:

Cals: 182	*Sodium: 661 mg*	*Calcium: 18 mg*
Total fat: 3.9 g	*Chol: 92 mg*	*Carbs: 1 g*
Sat fat: 1.1 g	*Fiber: <1 g*	*Protein: 34 g*

main dishes

tuscan chicken

The simple, rustic flavors of this fragrant dish blend beautifully with Easy, Delicious Swiss Chard or Mashed Potatoes with Turnips, Leeks and Horseradish.

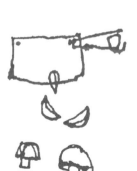

Olive oil cooking spray

1 tablespoon olive oil

2 large garlic cloves, coarsely chopped

1 tablespoon chopped fresh sage leaves

2 teaspoons chopped fresh rosemary

1 large leek, white and light green part only, coarsely chopped

4 (6- to 8-ounce) skinless chicken breast halves, bone-in

½ teaspoon salt, or to taste, and ground black pepper to taste

¼ teaspoon crushed red pepper

2 cups dry red wine

2 tablespoons tomato paste

1 bay leaf

8 ounces mushrooms, cleaned and quartered

Pre-prep: Chop garlic, sage, rosemary; trim root end and green leaves from leek, rinse thoroughly and chop; clean and quarter mushrooms.

1. Coat a large skillet with cooking spray, add the olive oil and place over medium heat. Add garlic, sage, rosemary and leek to hot skillet; reduce heat to low. Cook, stirring occasionally, until leek is tender and golden, about 10 minutes. (If leek begins to stick, cover skillet.)

2. Season the chicken with salt, black pepper and red pepper. Push aside the leek and add the chicken breasts to the skillet. Cook, uncovered, over moderately high heat, turning occasionally, for 10 minutes.

3. Add the wine and simmer over low heat until wine is reduced by half, about 10 minutes. Stir in tomato paste, bay leaf and mushrooms. Cover and simmer until the chicken is cooked through and is firm to the touch, about 10 minutes longer, being careful not to overcook. Discard bay leaf; spoon sauce over chicken.

Serves 4

Each serving has approximately:

Cals: 326	*Sodium: 403 mg*	*Calcium: 48 mg*
Total fat: 7.8 g	*Chol: 92 mg*	*Carbs: 9 g*
Sat fat: 1.6 g	*Fiber: 2 g*	*Protein: 35 g*

tip

Paste makes haste: Store leftover tomato paste in a zip-top freezer bag in the freezer for the next time you make a dish that calls for less than a can. Break it off in chunks or defrost in the microwave.

main dishes

raspberry beer chicken

Make the effort to find raspberry beer (or raspberry ginger ale). Combined with the strong, dark tea, it adds delightful raspberry notes to the sauce.

2 (12-ounce) bottles raspberry beer or raspberry ginger ale (divided use)

4 shallots, minced (divided use)

2 garlic cloves, minced

4 (6- to 8-ounce) skinless chicken breast halves, bone-in

½ teaspoon salt or to taste

Black pepper to taste

Olive oil cooking spray

1 tablespoon walnut oil

2 teaspoons minced fresh rosemary leaves

½ cup strong brewed tea (see note on Page 113)

½ cup fresh basil chiffonade (see Page 17)

Pre-prep: Make tea. Mince shallots, garlic and rosemary; chiffonade basil (see Page 17).

1. Mix 1 bottle of raspberry beer, 2 shallots and garlic in a medium non-reactive shallow container. Add the chicken breasts, salt and pepper. Marinate for at least 1 hour; if longer, refrigerate.

2. Coat a large skillet with cooking spray and place over low heat. Add walnut oil, remaining shallots and rosemary; cook, stirring, until shallots are translucent, about 2 minutes.

3. Remove chicken from marinade and discard marinade. Adjust heat to moderate, add chicken to the skillet, meaty side down. Cook, uncovered, for 5 to 6 minutes, turning chicken once.

4. When chicken is browned and shallots are golden, add ¾ cup of raspberry beer, cover and simmer 10 minutes.

5. Turn chicken, continue to simmer uncovered; liquid will reduce and darken in color. Gradually add remaining beer and reduce to about ¼ cup. After about 5 minutes the sauce will look like a thick coating on the skillet.

6. Add the strong tea to the skillet, boil until the remaining sauce has been reduced to about ½ cup and is dark and syrupy, about 1 or 2 more minutes.

7. To serve, place chicken on serving plate, sprinkle with basil chiffonade and drizzle about 2 tablespoons of the sauce over each serving.

Serves 4

Each serving has approximately:

Cals: 226	Sodium: 368 mg	Calcium: 33 mg
Total fat: 6.8 g	Chol: 80 mg	Carbs: 10 g
Sat fat: 1.3 g	Fiber: <1 g	Protein: 30 g

main dishes

rosemary–citrus snapper and peppers

Do the pre-prep steps for the marinade and main recipe together, as they have several ingredients in common. You'll find this aromatic marinade is similar to a paste.

rosemary citrus marinade

1 teaspoon grated lemon peel

1 teaspoon grated orange peel

2 tablespoons fresh lemon juice

2 cloves garlic, minced

1 teaspoon minced fresh rosemary

1 teaspoon dried thyme

1 tablespoon olive oil

Fresh ground pepper to taste

Pre-prep: Grate orange and lemon peel; juice lemon; mince garlic and rosemary.

Combine all ingredients.

---

4 (4-ounce) snapper steaks or other firm, mild fish, skin on one side

Rosemary Citrus Marinade (recipe at left)

Olive oil cooking spray

1 medium yellow or purple onion, cut in half lengthwise, then into slivers

2 large red bell peppers, seeded and cut into long strips

1 teaspoon frozen orange juice concentrate

1 teaspoon fresh minced rosemary

1 teaspoon grated orange peel

Salt and pepper to taste

6 green onions, sliced

⅓ cup Kalamata olives, pitted and sliced

2 tablespoons chopped parsley (divided use)

4 lemon wedges and 4 orange wedges (for garnish)

Pre-prep: Make marinade. Sliver onions; slice peppers; mince rosemary, grate orange peel; pit olives if you didn't buy them that way and slice; chop parsley; cut lemon and orange wedges.

1. Rinse fish and pat dry with a paper towel. Gently pat marinade into snapper; it will be like a paste. Set aside for 30 minutes.

2. While fish is marinating, heat a nonstick skillet over medium-high and coat with cooking spray. Add onions; cook, stirring occasionally, for 3 minutes.

3. Add the pepper strips, orange juice concentrate, rosemary, orange peel and salt and pepper to taste. Continue to cook over medium heat, stirring occasionally, about 7 minutes.

4. Add green onions and olives; stir and cook 1 minute longer. Remove to a bowl and allow to cool. Stir in 1 tablespoon parsley.

5. Prepare coals or heat a gas or electric grill on High. Spray grate with cooking spray. Add fish, skin side down; cover and cook 6 to 7 minutes.

6. To serve, divide the vegetables among 4 plates. Remove the skin from the fish, if desired. Place a steak on each plate. Garnish with remaining parsley and citrus wedges.

Makes 4 servings.

Each serving has approximately:

Cals: 204	*Chol: 42 mg*	*Calcium: 100 mg*
Total fat: 7 g	*Sodium: 269 mg*	*Carbs: 11 g*
Sat fat: 1 g	*Fiber: 1 g*	*Protein: 25 g*

main dishes

oven roasted tuna

S earing over high heat and finishing quickly in the oven is a classic restaurant technique for perfect fish.

4 (5-ounce) tuna steaks, about 1-inch thick	**Salt and freshly ground black pepper to taste**
Mustard Grilling Paste (see Page 82)	**Olive oil cooking spray**
2 teaspoons fresh lemon or lime juice	**2 tablespoons minced fresh herbs, such as basil, rosemary or parsley**

Pre-prep: Make grilling paste. Juice lemon or lime; mince herbs.

1. Preheat oven to 500° F. Mix grilling paste with lemon or lime juice. Season tuna steaks with salt and pepper, and coat 1 side with half of the grilling paste.

2. Spray a large, well-seasoned cast-iron skillet with cooking spray and place over high heat on a well-vented stove. Heat until skillet is smoking. Place the steaks, mustard-side down, into the hot, smoking skillet; cook them for 2 minutes without turning. Meanwhile, spread remaining grilling paste on the side facing up.

3. Carefully flip the steaks with a spatula and transfer the skillet to the oven. Bake for 5 to 6 minutes more or until fish is firm and still pink in the middle, like a medium steak. Remove skillet from oven and transfer steaks to serving plates. Sprinkle with fresh minced herbs.

Serves 4

Each serving has approximately:

Cals: 179	*Sodium: 132 mg*	*Calcium: 44 mg*
Total fat: 3.5 g	*Chol: 62 mg*	*Carbs: 2 g*
Sat fat: 0.5 g	*Fiber: <1 g*	*Protein: 33 g*

main dishes

risotto primavera
with shrimp and basil

You've had risotto before, but not only is this one divine, it doesn't require constant stirring.

20 large shrimp, peeled, deveined, butterflied (see note)

¾ cup Pernod or Sambuca liqueur

Olive oil cooking spray

¼ cup chopped onion

1 cup arborio rice

3½ cups nonfat, reduced-sodium chicken broth (divided use)

½ teaspoon salt

¾ cup fennel bulb, coarsely chopped

1 cup sugar snaps, or snow peas, cut in half (optional, see notes)

1 cup red pepper, cut in ¼-inch dice

1 large portobello mushroom sliced in strips, ¼x2-inches

½ cup basil chiffonade (divided use, see Page 17)

¼ cup grated Parmesan cheese

Pre-prep: Peel, devein and butterfly shrimp. Chop onion, fennel; prep sugar snaps or cut snow peas in half, if using; dice red pepper; cut mushroom into strips; chiffonade basil.

1. Place shrimp in a shallow container and cover with the liqueur.

2. Coat a medium saucepan with cooking spray and place over medium heat. When hot, add the onion and sauté for 1 minute.

3. Add the rice and stir in 2½ cups of broth and salt. Cover and cook for 10 minutes over medium heat, stirring 2 or 3 times. Uncover the pan and continue cooking and stirring, until all the stock has been absorbed.

4. Add the fennel, sugar snaps, if using, red pepper and another ½ cup of broth. Cook covered for 5 minutes, stirring once or twice.

5. Add the mushrooms and snow peas, if using, along with the remaining chicken broth. Cook, uncovered, stirring occasionally for another 5 minutes until creamy and rice is tender.

6. Remove the shrimp from the liqueur and reserve the liqueur. Coat a skillet with cooking spray and place over medium-high heat. Add the shrimp and quickly sauté, adding the reserved liqueur as necessary.

7. When shrimp are pink and firm, remove and add the remaining liqueur to the skillet. Over high heat, reduce the liqueur volume to half and stir in ¼ cup of the basil.

8. Meanwhile, stir Parmesan and remaining basil into the risotto. To serve, mound the risotto in the center of each dinner plate, stand 5 shrimp against the rice and drizzle the liqueur sauce over the shrimp.

Serves 4 to 6

Each serving has approximately:

Cals: 365	*Sodium: 626 mg*	*Calcium: 128 mg*
Total fat: 2.3 g	*Chol: 169 mg*	*Carbs: 17 g*
Sat. fat: 1 g	*Fiber: 1 g*	*Protein: 26 g*

note

The basic butterfly: To devein and butterfly peeled shrimp, cut a tiny slit from head end to tail, down the center of the back; flush with running water to remove vein. Cut again along the same line, about ¾ of the way through the flesh. Sides will open more when cooked to resemble a butterfly.

main dishes

ouzo shrimp with tomato, fennel and feta

Serve this over fluffy rice with complementary Orange Fennel Salad. Then, segue into Dark Chocolate Sorbet for dessert.

½ cup ouzo or Pernod liqueur

1 tablespoon olive oil

1 tablespoon dried oregano

½ tablespoon dried thyme

1½ pounds medium shrimp, peeled and deveined

Olive oil cooking spray

1 large purple onion, julienned

2 cloves garlic, minced

1 fresh fennel bulb, thinly sliced (about 1 cup)

1½ pounds Roma tomatoes, cut in ¾-inch chunks

½ teaspoon crushed red pepper or to taste

1 tablespoon minced fresh oregano or 1 additional teaspoon dried (optional)

4 ounces feta cheese

Pre-prep: Peel and devein shrimp. Julienne onion; mince garlic and fresh oregano, if using; slice fennel bulb; chunk tomatoes.

1. In glass or plastic container large enough to hold shrimp, mix ouzo, olive oil, dried oregano and thyme. Add shrimp and marinate, refrigerated, for 1 to 4 hours. Remove shrimp and reserve liquid.

2. Coat a heavy skillet with cooking spray, place over medium heat and sauté onions, garlic and fennel until tender, about 5 to 7 minutes; add reserved marinade. Reduce heat, cover and continue to cook about 5 more minutes. (Can be prepared to this point several hours ahead.) Just before serving, add tomatoes and crushed red pepper; cook 2 or 3 minutes.

3. Meanwhile, in another skillet coated with cooking spray, sauté shrimp until pink and firm, about 3 to 4 minutes. Add shrimp, dried oregano, if using, and feta cheese to tomato mixture; heat thoroughly, taking care that the tomatoes do not overcook . If using fresh oregano, sprinkle it on at the end.

Serves 4 to 6

Each serving has approximately:

Cals: 333   Sodium: 581 mg   Calcium: 213 mg
Total fat: 9.7 g   Chol: 286 mg   Carbs: 13 g
Sat fat: 4.2 g   Fiber: 3 g   Protein: 34 g

main dishes

grilled shrimp with cilantro pesto

B e sure to load the shrimp with pesto; some will fall off in the grill. Serve with Savory Corn Cakes and Carribean Salsa. Or chilled, turn Caesar Salad with Creamy Dressing into an entree.

Peel of 1 lemon

2 tablespoons lemon juice

1 tablespoon olive oil

1½ to 2 cups cilantro, leaves and stems, packed

2 large cloves garlic

2 shallots, peeled, rough cut

1½ pounds large shrimp, peeled and deveined

Olive oil cooking spray

Pre-prep: Remove lemon peel and juice lemon; peel and rough-cut shallots; peel and devein shrimp.

1. Place lemon peel in bowl of small food processor and process until uniform. Or, mince fine and place in a blender. Add the lemon juice, olive oil, cilantro, garlic and shallots; process until it reaches a pastelike consistency.

2. Thread shrimp onto skewers and coat both sides of shrimp with pesto paste. Marinate for 1 hour at room temperature or up to 2 hours in the refrigerator.

3. Prepare outdoor grill or a grill pan. If using gas, adjust grill to highest temperature. Spray grate with cooking spray and place skewers over high heat for 2 to 3 minutes on each side, until shrimp are pink and firm. Be careful not to overcook.

Serves 4

Each serving has approximately:

Cals: 211	*Sodium: 257 mg*	*Calcium: 114 mg*
Total fat: 5.3 g	*Chol: 258 mg*	*Carbs: 3 g*
Sat fat: 0.9 g	*Fiber: <1 g*	*Protein: 35 g*

note

If using bamboo skewers, soak in water about 20 minutes before skewering shrimp. For easier turning on the grill, thread shrimp onto 2 parallel skewers.

m a i n   d i s h e s

curried shrimp with basmati rice and peas

So many wonderful flavors, and they're intensified by the tofu. Fragrant, cumin-flecked rice and peas set off the brilliant sauce.

1 tablespoon butter

½ teaspoon red pepper flakes

½ teaspoon salt or to taste

1 teaspoon turmeric

½ teaspoon ground coriander

½ teaspoon ground cumin

1 teaspoon fresh ginger, minced

2 cloves garlic, minced

1 medium onion, finely chopped

1 pound medium shrimp, peeled and deveined

1 teaspoon honey

1 cup low-fat tofu blended with ½ cup water

2 tablespoons minced cilantro (divided use)

1 to 2 tablespoons lemon juice

1 tablespoon fresh mint leaves, minced (optional)

1 tablespoon cumin seeds

Butter-flavored cooking spray

2 cups cooked basmati rice

1 (10-ounce) package frozen peas, defrosted

Pre-prep: Cook rice. Mince ginger, garlic, cilantro and mint, if using; chop onion; peel and devein shrimp; blend tofu and water in blender; juice lemon.

1. Melt butter in a nonstick skillet over medium heat. Add pepper flakes, salt, turmeric, coriander and cumin. Stir and heat for about 1 minute. Add ginger, garlic and onion. Cover and cook until onion is translucent, about 5 minutes, stirring occasionally. Add 2 to 3 tablespoons water, if necessary, to prevent sticking.

2. Add the shrimp; cook, stirring, until shrimp are pink and nearly firm. Reduce heat to low.

3. Stir honey and blended tofu together, then add to shrimp mixture. Stir until well blended; continue to cook until simmering. Stir in cilantro, lemon juice and mint, if using. Remove from heat and cover to keep warm.

4. Meanwhile, in a heavy saucepan over medium heat, toast cumin seeds until fragrant, about 2 minutes, shaking often. Spray seeds with cooking spray. Add rice and stir to blend with cumin. Add peas on top. Reduce heat, cover and warm until peas are hot, about 5 minutes. Stir peas into rice.

5. To serve, divide rice among 4 plates and top with shrimp.

Serves 4

Each serving (with rice) has approximately:

Cals: 379	Sodium: 695 mg	Calcium: 120 mg
Total fat: 6 g	Chol: 230 mg	Carbs: 45 g
Sat fat: 2.5 g	Fiber: 6 g	Protein: 34 g

tip

Shrimply delicious: If you're a shrimp-lover, but watch the amount of cholesterol you eat, here's some good news: In a recent study, eating shrimp did raise blood cholesterol slightly, but it raised both LDL and HDL, so the all-important ratio was unchanged.

mediterranean frittata

Fresh flavors and a mosaic of vegetables make this open-face omelet a natural for brunch. Add some turkey sausage, muffins and your favorite Bloody Marys.

Olive oil cooking spray

2 teaspoons olive oil

1 red bell pepper, julienned

1 leek, white and light green part only, thinly sliced

2 cups spinach, chopped and packed

4 egg whites

2 whole eggs

½ cup light tofu, blended (see Page 17)

2 Roma tomatoes, thinly sliced

2 ounces feta cheese, finely crumbled

Finely minced fresh herbs, such as rosemary, basil and/or mint

¾ teaspoon salt, or to taste, and freshly ground black pepper to taste

Pre-prep: Julienne pepper; trim root end and green leaves from leek, rinse thoroughly and slice; rinse, dry and chop spinach; separate 4 eggs and reserve yolks for another use; blend tofu; slice tomatoes; mince herbs.

1. Preheat oven to 375° F. Coat a 10- to 12-inch oven-proof nonstick skillet with cooking spray and add olive oil; place over medium-high heat.

2. Add red pepper and leek, sauté until soft, then add spinach. Stir to mix and remove from heat.

3. Whisk egg whites, whole eggs and blended tofu together until well mixed; pour over vegetable mixture. Place skillet over medium heat and cook until sides of eggs begin to set.

4. Remove from heat, arrange tomato slices on top, sprinkle with feta and herbs; transfer skillet to oven; bake until eggs are set in center, about 10 to 15 minutes. Add salt and pepper to taste.

Serves 4

Each serving has approximately

Cals: 167	*Sodium: 739 mg*	*Calcium: 150 mg*
Total fat: 8.5 g	*Chol: 119 mg*	*Carbs: 11 g*
Sat fat: 1.2 g	*Fiber: 2 g*	*Protein: 13 g*

variation 1

Instead of red pepper, leek and spinach, mix in the skillet before adding egg mixture: ½ cup roasted corn, ¾ cup thinly sliced sun-dried tomatoes, 3 ounces cooked and crumbled turkey sausage and 2 tablespoons fresh thyme. Add eggs. Sprinkle more thyme and feta on top before transferring to oven. Serve with bottled marinara sauce.

variation 2

Instead of red pepper, leek and spinach, mix in the skillet before adding egg mixture: ½ purple onion, diced; 2 tablespoons chopped black olives; 3 sardines in tomato sauce, chopped; and 1 large tomato, diced. Add eggs. Sprinkle with fresh basil and oregano and feta before transferring to oven.

main dishes

thai veggie omelet

This is like an elegant stir-fry in an omelet, with the fresh Asian flavors ensconced in a fluffy egg wrapper. Side with basmati rice.

3 cloves garlic

8 black peppercorns

1 to 2 tablespoons cilantro stems

2 stalks lemon grass, cut in 1-inch pieces, or minced peel of 1 lemon (optional)

1 to 2 jalapeño peppers, seeded

Nonstick cooking spray

½ yellow or red bell pepper, julienned

1 to 2 tablespoons water, as needed

½ medium onion, julienned

1 cup snow peas, cut in 1-inch pieces

2 Roma tomatoes, seeded and diced

1 teaspoon sugar

Salt to taste

1 tablespoon Asian fish sauce

2 whole eggs

6 egg whites

2 tablespoons chopped cilantro leaves

Pre-prep: Remove leaves from cilantro stems, chop leaves; cut lemon grass or mince lemon peel, if using; seed jalapeño; julienne bell pepper and onion; cut snow peas; seed and dice tomatoes; separate eggs.

1. In a small food processor, puree garlic, peppercorns, cilantro stems, lemon grass or peel, if using, and jalapeño until finely minced.

2. Coat a wok or large skillet with cooking spray and stir-fry the pureed mixture for about 2 minutes over medium-high heat. Add the bell pepper, stirring, and cook about 2 more minutes; add 1 to 2 tablespoons water if vegetables start to stick.

3. Add onion and snow peas and stir, adding a little more water if needed. Lower heat, cover and cook vegetables just until soft, stirring occasionally. Add the tomatoes, sprinkle with sugar and remove from heat. Adjust to taste with salt.

4. Meanwhile, coat a 10-inch nonstick omelet pan with cooking spray and place over medium heat. Lightly beat fish sauce into eggs and egg whites. Pour egg mixture into hot omelet pan; reduce heat.

5. After about 30 seconds, use a spatula to lift the outside edge of the eggs, tilting the skillet to let the uncooked egg run under the cooked portion. Continue until only a thin layer of uncooked eggs remains on top.

6. Spoon part of the cooked vegetables evenly over the center of the omelet. Fold one side over the filling and gently slide the omelet onto a platter. Cut in half, place on individual serving plates and top with the remaining veggies. Sprinkle with cilantro leaves and serve.

Serves 2

Each entree-size serving has approximately:

Cals: 257	*Sodium: 883 mg*	*Calcium: 141 mg*
Total fat: 6.1 g	*Chol: 212 mg*	*Carbs: 29 g*
Sat fat: 1.7 g	*Fiber: 6 g*	*Protein: 23 g*

main dishes

beyond sauces

*salsas, dressings
and marinades*

beyond sauces: salsas, dressings and marinades

Brought up on sauces and gravies, we all love the way flavors spread through butter, pan drippings and cream. Were they not so lethal to hearts and thighs, who among us would exercise restraint, really? But beyond buerre blanc and bechemel, opulent flavors and textures beguile in their own way. Salsas, with their crunchiness and sweet-hot tartness, turn fish and chicken on, especially when matched with spicy counterpoint. Just try Chile-Rubbed Pan-Fried Chicken with Mango-Cilantro Salsa or Jicama-Red Pepper Salsa. Simple, big-flavored combinations like Raspberry Dressing and mustardy Creole Dressing lift greens out of the ordinary. And a condiment like Spiced Kumquat Chutney transforms a handheld wrapper into a minor masterpiece. With the exception of salsas, most of these recipes use oil; the point isn't no-fat, but lower fat, better fat. And big, fat flavor.

jicama-red pepper salsa

This light, refreshing salsa adds pizzazz to Chile-Rubbed Pan-Fried Chicken, grilled fish — even green salad.

Juice of 1½ limes

1 tablespoon sugar

1 teaspoon frozen orange juice concentrate

2 cups peeled and julienned jicama

½ red bell pepper, finely chopped

¼ cup chopped cilantro

Pre-prep: Juice limes; peel and julienne jicama; chop red bell pepper and cilantro.

Mix lime juice, sugar and orange juice concentrate. Combine jicama, red pepper and cilantro; toss gently in lime juice dressing. Serve immediately or refrigerate for up to 2 days. Note: If you don't plan to serve this right away, reserve cilantro and add just before serving.

Serves 4

Each serving has approximately:

Cals: 54
Total fat: None
Sat fat: None

Sodium: 5 mg
Chol: None
Fiber: 4 g

Calcium: 17 mg
Carbs: 13 g
Protein: 1 g

pear and red onion salsa

This fresh-tasting, minty salsa adds zest to poultry – and even lamb. Pass it at Thanksgiving as an alternative to cranberry sauce.

1 small red onion, chopped

¼ cup chopped fresh mint

3 tablespoons fresh lime juice

3 jalapeño peppers, seeded and finely minced

1 tablespoon brown sugar

2 teaspoons minced fresh ginger

3 large Bosc pears, cored and chopped

Pre-prep: Chop onion and mint; juice limes; mince peppers and ginger; chop pears.

Combine all ingredients and stir gently to blend. Serve within 1 hour.

Serves 12

Each ¼ cup serving has approximately:

Cals: 30
Total fat: 0.3 g
Sat fat: None

Sodium: 1 mg
Chol: None
Fiber: 1 g

Calcium: 8 mg
Carbs: 7 g
Protein: <1 g

beyond sauces

mango–cilantro salsa

Serve this bright tropical salsa over grilled chicken or fish, or spoon onto mixed greens as a combination dressing and garnish. To turn up the heat, add some minced jalapeño or a dash of hot pepper sauce.

1 large mango, diced (see Page 17)

1 medium red bell pepper, diced

1 medium purple onion, diced

1 to 2 tablespoons lime juice or rice wine vinegar

2 tablespoons coarsely chopped cilantro leaves

2 tablespoons unsweetened grated coconut (optional)

Pre-prep: Dice mango, pepper and onion; juice limes; chop cilantro.

Mix all ingredients together. Serve immediately or refrigerate for several hours.

Serves 6

Each serving has approximately:

Cals: 52	*Sodium: 4 mg*	*Calcium: 17 mg*
Total fat: 0.7 g	*Chol: None*	*Carbs: 12 g*
Sat fat: 0.5 g	*Fiber: 1 g*	*Protein: 1 g*

spicy caribbean salsa

Serve this tropical refresher with Chile-Rubbed Pan-Fried Chicken, grilled seafood or as a dip with flavored tortilla chips.

1 cup papaya, peeled, seeded and diced

1 tomato, peeled, seeded and diced

¼ cup chopped cilantro

1½ tablespoons fresh lime juice

1 teaspoon olive oil

Carribean hot pepper sauce

Pre-prep: Peel, seed and dice papaya and tomato; chop cilantro; juice limes.

Combine papaya, tomato, cilantro, lime juice and olive oil in medium bowl and gently mix. Season to taste with hot pepper sauce. Salsa can be prepared 3 hours ahead; cover and refrigerate.

Serves 4

Each serving has approximately:

Cals: 32	*Sodium: 10 mg*	*Calcium: 13 mg*
Total fat: 1.3 g	*Chol: None*	*Carbs: 5 g*
Sat fat: 0.2 g	*Fiber: 1 g*	*Protein: 1 g*

southwest black-eyed pea spread

Serve this smooth, chile-spiked spread with tortilla chips or pita triangles. It's also surprisingly good made with canned soybeans.

2 garlic cloves

1 jalapeño pepper, stem and seeds removed

1 (15-ounce) can black-eyed peas, drained

2 tablespoons sesame tahini

1 tablespoon lemon juice

1 teaspoon chili powder

1 teaspoon ground cumin

Freshly ground black pepper

Cayenne pepper to taste (optional)

1 to 2 tablespoons warm water, as needed, for consistency

Fresh chopped cilantro for garnish

Pre-prep: Remove pepper stem and seeds; juice lemon; chop cilantro.

1. With food processor motor running, drop in garlic cloves and jalapeño pepper. Add black-eyed peas, tahini and lemon juice. Process until smooth and creamy, pausing to scrape down the sides of the bowl.

2. Add chili powder, cumin, black pepper and cayenne, if using; continue to process. Add water to thin, if necessary.

3. This tastes best after refrigerating 2 hours to blend flavors. Garnish with a sprinkle of cilantro.

Serves 8

Each serving has approximately:

Cals: 55	*Sodium: 242 mg*	*Calcium: 27 mg*
Total fat: 2 g	*Chol: None*	*Carbs: 8 g*
Sat fat: 0.3 g	*Fiber: 2 g*	*Protein: 3 g*

tip

Chop talk: When chopping garlic in a large food processor, start the motor first, then drop in the garlic before adding other ingredients. This way, it will be more thoroughly minced. Also, make sure the processor bowl is dry, or food will stick to it instead of getting minced.

beyond sauces

white bean and basil bruschetta

Heating the liquids and herbs before combining with the beans coaxes out the wonderful Mediterranean flavors.

1 (15.5-ounce) can Great Northern beans, rinsed and drained

1 tablespoon extra-virgin olive oil

2 tablespoons red-wine vinegar

2 tablespoons balsamic vinegar

1 tablespoon lemon juice

2 tablespoons Dijon mustard

2 teaspoons minced garlic

2 teaspoons sugar

1 teaspoon salt or to taste

Freshly ground black pepper

$\frac{1}{4}$ cup finely minced fresh basil

3 Roma tomatoes, seeded and cut in $\frac{1}{4}$-inch dice

1 small purple onion, cut in $\frac{1}{4}$-inch dice

1 (16-ounce) French baguette, cut in $\frac{1}{2}$-inch slices

Olive oil cooking spray

Pre-prep: Rinse and drain beans. Juice lemon; mince garlic and basil; seed tomatoes and dice; dice onion; slice baguette.

1. Mash half the beans with a fork; mix in the whole beans.

2. In a small, microwave-proof bowl, mix together oil, vinegars, lemon juice, mustard, garlic, sugar, salt and pepper. Heat 1 minute on High (100% power) in the microwave to blend flavors; pour over the beans and stir to mix.

3. Preheat oven to 400° F. After beans have cooled to room temperature, gently stir in the basil, tomatoes and onion.

4. Lightly coat the bread on both sides with cooking spray. Place in oven for 6 to 7 minutes to toast. Heap the bean mixture onto the bread slices and serve.

Serves 12

Each serving (2 bruschetta) has approximately:

Cals: 159   Sodium: 441 mg   Calcium: 57 mg
Total fat: 2.6 g   Chol: None   Carbs: 28 g
Sat fat: 0.4 g   Fiber: 3 g   Protein: 6 g

tip

Iron boost: Eating a vitamin C-rich food (like tomatoes) with a non-meat source of iron (like beans) will increase iron absorption.

beyond sauces

phytopia pesto

Kale scores so high for nutrients, but who knows how to serve it? This pesto is a charmer; guests never know they're eating kale, but love the fresh greenness. Serve over pasta, on bruschetta – even as a spread on wrappers and quesadillas.

¾ pound kale, washed, large stems removed

3 to 4 cloves garlic, peeled

¾ cup basil leaves

Juice of 1 lemon

2 tablespoons olive oil

1 teaspoon salt, or to taste, and freshly ground black pepper

Extra-virgin olive oil (optional)

Pre-prep: Wash and stem kale; stem basil; juice lemon.

1. Coarsely chop kale, leaving water on leaves from washing. Place in large microwavable bowl and cover. Microwave on High (100% power) for 5 minutes. Stir; return to microwave for another 5 minutes. Let stand 2 to 3 minutes; remove cover to cool.

2. Drop garlic into the bowl of a food processor with the motor running. When finely minced, add the basil and cooked kale. Process until uniform.

3. Add lemon juice, olive oil, salt and pepper to taste. Serve as you would pesto. Drizzle with olive oil, if you like.

Serves 4

Each serving has approximately:

Cals: 114	*Sodium: 616 mg*	*Calcium: 122 mg*
Total fat: 7 g	*Chol: None*	*Carbs: 10 g*
Sat fat: 1 g	*Fiber: 5 g*	*Protein: 3 g*

serving suggestion

Cook 1 pound pasta, preferably fusilli, penne or another kind that holds chunky sauces well; drain and reserve cooking water. Return pasta to pan. Toast 4 tablespoons pine nuts (see Page 17); set aside. Chop 3 to 4 ripe medium tomatoes; heat just until warm in the microwave. Add a little pasta cooking liquid, pesto, tomatoes and 4 ounces crumbled feta to the pasta and toss to mix. Divide among 4 plates; garnish with pine nuts and drizzle with olive oil, if desired.

beyond sauces

balsamic vinaigrette

This basic dressing brings out the best in a salad of romaine and red leaf lettuce, garden-ripe tomatoes and freshly pulled onions.

1/3 cup balsamic vinegar

3 tablespoons cream sherry

2 cloves garlic, minced

1 or 2 shallots, finely minced

1½ tablespoons extra-virgin olive oil or basil-flavored olive oil

¾ teaspoon anchovy paste

1 tablespoon chopped fresh mint (optional)

¼ teaspoon salt, or to taste, and ground pepper to taste

Combine all ingredients and mix thoroughly.

Serves 4

Each serving has approximately:

Cals: 90	*Sodium: 187 mg*	*Calcium: 8 mg*
Total fat: 5 g	*Chol: 1 mg*	*Carbs: 7 g*
Sat fat: 0.7 g	*Fiber: None*	*Protein: <1 g*

pink peppercorn reduction

This spicy, faintly sweet sauce is excellent with oven-roasted salmon, and it adds sparkle to almost any fish, poultry or beef entree.

1 cup dry red wine

1 cup port wine

1½ teaspoons pink peppercorns, crushed (see note)

2 teaspoons seedless raspberry or red currant jelly

1½ teaspoon prepared horseradish

1 to 2 tablespoons minced fresh herbs, such as thyme, rosemary or basil

¼ teaspoon salt or to taste

Pre-prep: Crush peppercorns with mortar and pestle; mince herbs.

1. Place wines, peppercorns, jelly and horseradish in a small skillet over high heat.

2. Boil until volume is reduced to about ¾ cup, about 15 minutes; it should be syruplike. Stir in the fresh herbs and salt.

Serves 4

Each serving has approximately:

Cals: 145	*Sodium: 157 mg*	*Calcium: 13 mg*
Total fat: 0.4 g	*Chol: 1 mg*	*Carbs: 11 g*
Sat fat: 0.2 g	*Fiber: None*	*Protein: <1 g*

note

Pink peppercorns have a soft, luminous aroma reminiscent of eucalyptus or juniper. Unlike hard black peppercorns, their paperlike skins crush easily.

beyond sauces

ginger-sesame dressing

For a refreshing Asian take on salad, toss this fragrant, slightly sweet dressing with Napa cabbage, bean sprouts, tomatoes and green onions. Or drizzle it over grilled veggies and rice.

1 tablespoon minced fresh ginger

1 tablespoon minced garlic

½ cup balsamic vinegar

¼ cup red wine vinegar

¼ cup reduced-sodium soy sauce

1½ tablespoons honey

1 teaspoon Dijon mustard

2 teaspoons sesame oil

Mince ginger and garlic, combine with remaining ingredients.

Serves 4

Each serving has approximately:

Cals: 65
Total fat: 2.4 g
Sat fat: 0.3 g

Sodium: 615 mg
Chol: None
Fiber: None

Calcium: 18 mg
Carbs: 9 g
Protein: 1 g

spiced kumquat chutney

For a festive holiday touch, serve this chutney in hollowed-out orange or lemon halves or in tiny pumpkins. It adds wonderful zest to roast poultry or turkey sandwiches.

12 ounces kumquats, quartered lengthwise and seeded

1 cup sugar

¾ cup orange juice

½ cup dried cranberries or currants

¼ cup chopped shallots

1½ tablespoons minced fresh ginger

½ teaspoon ground star anise (see note)

¼ teaspoon ground black pepper

¼ teaspoon ground anise seed

¼ teaspoon ground cinnamon

¼ teaspoon ground cloves

Pre-prep: Quarter and seed kumquats; chop shallots; mince ginger.

Combine all ingredients in a medium, heavy saucepan over high heat; bring to a boil. Continue to boil, stirring occasionally, until the kumquat skins are tender and the mixture begins to thicken slightly, about 15 to 20 minutes. Transfer to a bowl and chill. May be made 3 to 4 days ahead.

Serves 8

Each serving has approximately:

Cals: 169
Total fat: 0.1 g
Sat fat: None

Sodium: 6 mg
Chol: None
Fiber: 4 g

Calcium: 29 mg
Carbs: 43 g
Protein: 1 g

note

If only whole spices are available, grind with a mortar and pestle or in a small food processor or substitute 1½ teaspoons Chinese 5-spice powder for spices.

beyond sauces

poppy seed dressing

Tofu strikes again, this time in a creamy version of classic poppy seed dressing. Use it on a spinach salad with grapefruit or orange sections, or on mesclun greens.

½ cup light and firm silken tofu

3 tablespoons apple cider vinegar

6 tablespoons sugar

½ teaspoon Dijon mustard

2 teaspoons coarsely chopped onion

2 teaspoons poppy seeds

½ teaspoon salt or to taste

Blend the tofu, vinegar, sugar, mustard and onion in a food processor or blender until creamy. Stir in poppy seeds and salt; mix well.

Serves 6

Each serving has approximately:

Cals: 55
Total fat: 0.5 g
Sat fat: None

Sodium: 197 mg
Chol: None
Fiber: None

Calcium: 15 mg
Carbs: 13 g
Protein: <1 g

raspberry dressing

Pink peppercorns suffuse this dressing with exquisite spiciness. Double or triple the recipe to keep on hand for greens or fruit.

2 teaspoons pink peppercorns

2 shallots, minced

½ cup rice vinegar

1½ tablespoons seedless raspberry jam

1 teaspoon frozen white grape juice concentrate

1 tablespoon canola oil

Salt to taste

Pre-prep: Crush peppercorns with mortar and pestle. Alternatively, put peppercorns in a heavy plastic bag and crush with a rolling pin. Mince shallots.

Combine all ingredients and mix thoroughly.

Serves 4

Each serving has approximately:

Cals: 60
Total fat: 3.4 g
Sat fat: 0.3 g

Sodium: 586 mg
Chol: None
Fiber: <1 g

Calcium: 11 mg
Carbs: 8 g
Protein: <1 g

beyond sauces

orange-basil marinade

This bright, citrus- and herb-spiked marinade is especially delicious on chicken or seafood. This makes 1 cup marinade, enough for 4 servings of chicken or fish.

½ cup dry white wine or vermouth

¼ cup frozen orange juice concentrate

1 tablespoon chopped fresh rosemary

2 tablespoons chopped fresh basil

1 tablespoon grated orange peel

1 teaspoon canola oil

Freshly ground black pepper

Pre-prep: Chop rosemary and basil; grate orange peel.

Combine all ingredients in a shallow plastic or glass pan and add skinless, boneless chicken breast or seafood, in a single layer. Cover and refrigerate for 1 to 4 hours.

Serves 4

Cals: 61
Total fat: 1.2 g
Sat fat: 0.1 g

Sodium: 2 mg
Chol: None
Fiber: <1 g

Calcium: 17 mg
Carbs: 8 g
Protein: 0.5 g

vietnamese lemon grass marinade

For a subtle Asian note, use this marinade on seafood or chicken. Reserve and boil it to use as a sauce. This makes 1 cup marinade, enough for 4 servings of chicken or fish.

1 to 2 stalks lemon grass

2 to 3 cloves garlic

2 to 3 tablespoons Asian fish sauce

2 teaspoons sugar

Juice from ½ lime

1 teaspoon canola oil

Pre-prep: Remove and discard fibrous parts from lemon grass; cut into 1-inch lengths; juice lime.

Combine all ingredients in a blender or small food processor. Marinate chicken or seafood for up to 2 hours refrigerated. Discard marinade.

Serves 4

Cals: 37
Total fat: 1.3 g
Sat fat: Trace

Sodium: 450 mg
Chol: None
Fiber: <1 g

Calcium: 34 mg
Carbs: 6 g
Protein: 1 g

tip

Lemon grass: Buy fresh lemon grass when you can. So you never get caught short, chop any left over into 1-inch lengths and store in a zip-top freezer bag in the freezer to use as needed.

beyond sauces

beyond sauces

mustard grilling paste

Any combination of fresh herbs, such as basil, rosemary or tarragon, may be substituted for the green peppercorns and capers in this versatile grilling paste. Use what's on hand.

3 tablespoons Dijon mustard

1 tablespoon green peppercorns

1 tablespoon capers

1 teaspoon canola or olive oil

Freshly ground black pepper

Puree all ingredients together in a small food processor or with a handheld blender. Use to coat tuna, salmon, swordfish, chicken breasts or pork or beef tenderloin. Spread on all sides. Cook fish or meat directly on a hot, well-seasoned grill or, alternatively, lay it on foil punched with holes on grill.

Serves 4

Each serving has approximately:

Cals: 25
Total fat: 2 g
Sat fat: 0.1 g

Sodium: 222
Chol: None
Fiber: <1 g

Calcium: 16 mg
Carbs: 1 g
Protein: 1 g

minute marinades

Use the following formula to make quick marinades with the dominant flavors of your choice. This makes enough for 4 servings:

1 teaspoon to 1 tablespoon oil

¼ cup liquid, such as vinegar and/or juices

1 teaspoon dried herbs (or 1 tablespoon fresh, chopped)

1 to 2 cloves crushed garlic

Asian: Sesame oil, rice vinegar, ginger, garlic.

Greek: Extra-virgin olive oil, lemon juice, oregano (preferably Greek), garlic.

Italian: Extra-virgin olive oil, red wine vinegar, oregano and rosemary, garlic.

French: Extra-virgin olive oil, red wine vinegar, dried *herbes de Provençe* and garlic.

Southwest: Canola or olive oil, lime juice and orange juice, chili powder, garlic.

tip

Glass act: Always use glass or plastic containers for marinating because acid can react with some metals and change the flavor.

salads

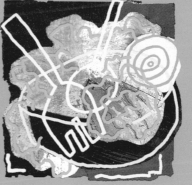

sensational sides: salads

When a main salad doesn't fit the menu, it's still possible to incorporate a smaller-scale salad component, whether it's a trimmed-down, cranked-up Caesar or a Green Bean Salad as fresh as a Mediterranean wave. And for sheer indulgence, what could be naughtier than strawberries, kiwi, mango and greens tossed with macadamia vinaigrette? The point of such combinations is to broaden your repertoire of fruits and vegetables, working elements such as goat cheese and macadamias for maximum flavor. In small amounts, they're magical.

spinach, oranges and pine nuts with tarragon-mustard vinaigrette

In the winter, fire up your taste buds with this elegant variation on spinach salad.

2 blood oranges or seedless oranges, peeled (see note on Page 93)

1 (10-ounce) bag spinach, rinsed, stems removed and torn

8 ounces mushrooms, sliced

Tarragon-Mustard Vinaigrette (recipe at left)

2 tablespoons toasted pine nuts (see Page 17)

Pre-prep: Make dressing; peel oranges (see note on page 93); rinse and dry spinach, remove stems, tear; clean and slice mushrooms; toast pine nuts (see Page 17).

1. Cut 1 orange into 1-inch cubes; cut the remaining orange into horizontal slices about ¼-inch thick.

2. In a large bowl, place spinach, mushrooms and orange cubes. Add dressing, toss and place on serving plates; garnish with orange slices and toasted pine nuts.

Serves 4

Each serving has approximately:

Cals: 139	*Sodium: 98 mg*	*Calcium: 116 mg*
Total fat: 5.6 g	*Chol: None*	*Carbs: 20 mg*
Sat fat: 0.8 g	*Fiber: 5 g*	*Protein: 6 g*

tarragon mustard vinaigrette

3 tablespoons orange juice concentrate

2 teaspoons Worcestershire sauce

¼ cup rice vinegar

1 tablespoon cream sherry

2 teaspoons sesame or walnut oil

1 tablespoon dried tarragon or 2 tablespoons fresh minced tarragon

2 teaspoons Dijon mustard

In a small bowl, mix all ingredients together.

sides . . salads

summer salad with berries and macadamia vinaigrette

This salad is so cool in the summer, especially if you happen to have a veranda handy. Toasting nuts, from almonds to macadamias, brings out their flavor.

2 tablespoons lightly salted macadamia nuts, toasted (divided use, see Page 17)

2 shallots

½ cup rice vinegar

2 tablespoons white grape juice concentrate

½ teaspoon salt

2 teaspoons canola oil or macadamia nut oil

8 cups mixed greens or mesclun

8 large strawberries, sliced (see note)

1 small mango, peeled and cubed

1 kiwi, peeled and sliced

Pre-prep: Toast nuts (see Page 17); rinse, dry and tear greens; slice strawberries; peel and slice mango and kiwi.

1. Finely mince half the nuts in a small food processor with the shallots. Transfer to a small bowl; mix in rice vinegar, grape juice concentrate, salt and oil. Chop remaining nuts and set aside.

2. Reserving 2 tablespoons, pour dressing over the greens and toss. Place greens on serving plate and arrange berries, mango and kiwi on top. Drizzle fruit with remaining dressing and sprinkle with remaining nuts.

Serves 4

Each serving has approximately:

Cals: 154	*Sodium: 338 mg*	*Calcium: 77 mg*
Total fat: 7.4 g	*Chol: None*	*Carbs: 21 g*
Sat fat: 0.8 g	*Fiber: 4 g*	*Protein: 3 g*

sides: salads

note

Here are some other seasonal possibilities for the fruit:

Winter: Orange and/or purple onion, thinly sliced

Fall: Apples or pears, thinly sliced (do not peel)

mixed greens and fruit with raspberry-walnut vinaigrette

This simple-sounding salad is just so good, especially the way the dressing complements the fruit. The nuts give wonderful crunch.

2 cups romaine lettuce, torn into bite-size pieces

2 cups red leaf lettuce, torn into bite-size pieces

2 cups butter lettuce, torn into bite-size pieces

1 cup thinly sliced radicchio

Raspberry-Walnut Vinaigrette (recipe at left)

2¼ cups sliced pears and red onions

4 teaspoons sliced almonds, toasted (see Page 17)

Pre-Prep: Make vinaigrette. Rinse, dry and tear lettuces; slice radicchio; rinse and prepare fruit; toast almonds and chop (see Page 17).

1. Place lettuces and radicchio in a large salad bowl. Add dressing, reserving about ¼ cup, and toss gently.

2. Divide dressed greens among 4 salad plates; arrange fruit on top. Drizzle some of the remaining dressing over each salad; sprinkle with almonds and serve immediately.

Serves 4

Each serving has approximately:

Cals: 198	*Sodium: 76 mg*	*Calcium: 80 mg*
Total fat: 9 g	*Chol: None*	*Carbs: 26 g*
Sat fat: 0.8 g	*Fiber: 4 g*	*Protein: 3 g*

raspberry walnut vinaigrette

1 tablespoon pink peppercorns

2 large shallots, finely minced

¼ cup orange juice concentrate

2 tablespoons cream sherry

1½ tablespoons white Worcestershire sauce

2 teaspoons raspberry preserves

2 teaspoons Dijon mustard

White pepper to taste

2 tablespoons walnut oil

¼ cup rice vinegar

1. Crush pink peppercorns with a mortar and pestle or in a spice grinder; transfer to a small bowl.

2. Add remaining ingredients, and mix well.

sides: salads

apple, pear and goat cheese salad

This salad is wonderful when the first crisp days of fall roll around, and tofu makes the decadence of the cheese go farther.

2 tablespoons goat cheese, blue or Roquefort cheese

2 tablespoons light and firm silken tofu, blended (see Page 17)

6 cups mixed greens (see note)

1 Granny Smith apple, cored and cut into ⅛x1-inch pieces

1 small red onion, julienned

Apple-Walnut Vinaigrette (recipe at right)

1 firm, ripe Bosc or Anjou pear, cored and thinly sliced

2 tablespoons chopped toasted almonds (optional, see Page 17)

Pre-prep: Make vinaigrette. Blend tofu and toast almonds, if using (see Page 17). Rinse, dry and tear greens; julienne onion; core and cut apple and pear; chop almonds, if using.

1. Mix goat cheese and blended tofu until smooth and creamy. If you can't bring yourself to use tofu, substitute nonfat sour cream. (This can be done in advance and refrigerated.)

2. Just before serving, toss greens, apple pieces and onion with vinaigrette, reserving a small amount to drizzle over the finished salad.

3. Divide the greens among 4 salad plates; arranging pear slices on top with a dollop of the cheese mixture. Drizzle with remaining vinaigrette; top with toasted almonds, if using, and serve immediately.

Serves 4

Each serving has approximately:

Cals:196	*Sodium: 396 mg*	*Calcium: 105 mg*
Total fat: 6.3 g	*Chol: 3 mg*	*Carbs: 32 g*
Sat fat: 1.4 g	*Fiber: 4 g*	*Protein: 4 g*

---

apple walnut vinaigrette

2 cloves garlic

2 small shallots

¼ cup frozen apple juice concentrate

1½ tablespoons white Worcestershire sauce

¼ cup rice vinegar

2 teaspoons dried oregano

½ teaspoon salt

½ teaspoon dry mustard

1 tablespoon walnut oil

1. Finely mince garlic and shallots in a food processor or blender.

2. Add remaining ingredients and mix well.

note

Here are two possibilities for the greens: 5 cups mixed greens (such as red leaf or butter lettuce, spinach or arugula) and 1 cup radicchio leaves; or 4 cups mesclun greens mixed with 2 cups torn red leaf lettuce.

sides: salads

southwest chopped salad with black bean dressing

Even the lettuce is chopped in this vibrant, chunky salad, which pairs well with Jalapeño-Pumpkin Seed Quesadillas. You'll have room for dessert — Bananas Diablo.

1 large head red leaf lettuce, separated into leaves, rinsed and dried

¾ cup red cabbage, chopped into 1-inch cubes

2 large tomatoes, cubed

1 medium red onion, finely chopped

½ cup roasted corn kernels (optional, see page 17)

Black Bean Dressing (recipe at left)

¼ cup jicama or radish, julienned, for garnish (optional)

Pre-prep: Rinse and dry lettuce; cube cabbage and tomatoes; roast corn, if using; chop onion; julienne jicama or radish, if using.

1. Stack about one-fourth of the lettuce leaves with all stems pointing in the same direction. Start at one side and roll into a long tube. With a sharp knife, cut ribbons about ⅜-inch wide. Continue with remaining lettuce leaves.

2. Toss lettuce in a large bowl with cabbage, tomatoes, onion and corn. Add salad dressing just before serving and toss. Garnish each serving with jicama or radish, if desired.

Serves 4

Each serving has approximately:

Cals: 103	*Sodium: 62 mg*	*Calcium: 97 mg*
Total fat: 4 g	*Chol: None*	*Carbs: 14 g*
Sat fat: 0.5 g	*Fiber: 4 g*	*Protein: 3 g*

black bean dressing

2 cloves garlic

2 tablespoons nonfat black bean dip

1 tablespoon olive oil

2 tablespoons frozen orange juice concentrate

⅓ cup red wine vinegar

2 teaspoons ground cumin

1 teaspoon chili powder

½ teaspoon ground oregano

1 teaspoon Worcestershire sauce

Mince garlic, then mix all ingredients in a small bowl.

harvey's caesar salad

Harv's truly an artist when it comes to his Caesar — done by taste, not formula. His always turns out flawless, but developing a recipe took us nearly two years.

25 black peppercorns, crushed, or
¾ teaspoon freshly ground pepper

¾ teaspoon anchovy paste

1 tablespoon Worcestershire sauce

4 cloves garlic, minced

1 teaspoon dry mustard

Juice of ½ lemon

2 teaspoons red wine vinegar

2 tablespoons cream sherry

2 tablespoons canola or olive oil

6 to 8 cups romaine lettuce, torn

2 tablespoons shredded Parmesan cheese

Pre-prep: Crush or grind pepper. Mince garlic; juice lemon. Rinse, dry and tear lettuce. Shred cheese.

1. In a small bowl, mix pepper, anchovy paste, Worcestershire sauce, garlic, mustard, lemon juice, vinegar, cream sherry and oil until well blended.

2. Place lettuce in a large salad bowl; toss with dressing and half of the cheese.

3. Divide salad on serving plates; sprinkle each with a small amount of cheese and serve.

Serves 4

Each serving has approximately:

Cals: 118 *Sodium: 156 mg* *Calcium: 83 mg*
Total fat: 8.8 g *Chol: 5 mg* *Carbs: 5 g*
Sat fat: 1.2 g *Fiber: 2 g* *Protein: 4 g*

sides: salads

caesar salad with creamy dressing

How many permutations can there be on the bold, basic Caesar? This one's a wee bit lower in fat, but the way tofu cranks up the garlic, it's an unabashed vampire-blaster.

1 clove garlic, crushed

¾ teaspoon anchovy paste

2 teaspoons extra-virgin olive oil

2 teaspoons lemon juice

1 tablespoon red wine vinegar

1 teaspoon Worcestershire sauce

1 teaspoon Dijon mustard

2 tablespoons buttermilk or skim milk

¼ cup light and firm silken tofu, blended (see Page 17)

8 cups torn romaine lettuce

2 tablespoons grated Parmesan cheese

½ teaspoon freshly ground black pepper or to taste

1 cup croutons (optional, recipe at left)

Pre-prep: Make croutons. Crush garlic; blend tofu; juice lemon; rinse, dry and tear romaine.

1. Mix garlic and anchovy paste in a small bowl. Add olive oil, lemon juice, vinegar, Worcestershire, mustard and buttermilk; mix well. Stir in blended tofu.

2. Place lettuce in a large salad bowl; add cheese and black pepper. Pour dressing over salad and toss gently to coat. Top with croutons and serve immediately.

Serves 4

Each serving has approximately:

Cals: 70
Total fat: 3.8 g
Sat fat: 0.8 g

Sodium: 170 mg
Chol: 4 mg
Fiber: 3 g

Calcium: 102 mg
Carbs: 5 g
Protein: 7 g

croutons

Preheat oven to 400° F. Cut 2 slices bread (white, whole wheat or multi-grain) into ½-inch cubes. Place in a baking pan; lightly coat the cubes with olive oil cooking spray. Dust with garlic powder or add fresh minced garlic, if desired. Bake for 5 minutes, stir, and continue to bake an additional 2 minutes. Remove from the oven and allow to cool. Cubes should be crisp; if not, return to oven for an additional minute or two.

hot 'n' coleslaw

For the most authentic version of this exquisite hot-and-sour Asian slaw, use the optional ingredients. If it's too spicy, reduce or even sack the chiles.

1 pound savoy cabbage, shredded, or 1 (16-ounce) bag coleslaw mix

½ cup cilantro, basil and/or mint leaves, chopped

1 medium purple onion, julienned, or 6 small green onions, thinly sliced

½ cup daikon radish, julienned or coarsely grated (optional)

2 stalks lemon grass, finely minced (optional)

Thai Salad Dressing (recipe at right)

4 large red leaf lettuce leaves

3 to 4 firm, ripe tomatoes, sliced in wedges

2 small cucumbers, thinly sliced

Pre-prep: Prepare dressing. Shred cabbage; chop fresh herbs; julienne onion and radish, if using; mince lemon grass, if using; rinse and dry lettuce leaves; slice tomatoes and cucumbers.

1. Layer cabbage, chopped herbs (reserve 2 tablespoons for garnish), onion, radish and lemon grass, if using, in a large salad bowl.

2. Pour dressing over salad and toss to mix well. (The easy way is to use a bowl with a tight-fitting lid and turn the bowl several times.)

3. When ready to serve, place lettuce leaves on 4 serving plates and mound with cabbage. Arrange tomato and cucumber on the plates; garnish with reserved herbs.

Serves 4

Each serving has approximately:

Cals: 107	*Sodium: 931 mg*	*Calcium: 107 mg*
Total fat: 0.7 g	*Chol: None*	*Carbs: 25 g*
Sat fat: None	*Fiber: 4 g*	*Protein: 4 g*

thai salad dressing

3 large cloves garlic

4 green serrano chiles, seeded

4 small, hot Thai chiles, seeded

Juice of 3 limes (about ⅓ cup)

¼ cup Asian fish sauce

2 tablespoons water

3 tablespoons sugar

1. In a small food processor or using mortar and pestle, crush the garlic and chiles.

2. Transfer to a small bowl; add the remaining ingredients and mix well.

sides: salads

orange and fennel salad

With bright citrus, delicate fennel and bold greens, this salad beats the winter doldrums.

4 large, firm, juicy oranges, peeled (see note)

1 large fennel bulb

$\frac{1}{3}$ cup red wine vinegar

$\frac{1}{4}$ cup frozen orange juice concentrate

2 teaspoons dried oregano, crumbled

2 teaspoons extra-virgin olive oil

1 large bunch watercress, about 3 cups of leaves

4 ounces spinach, about 3 cups leaves (tear if large)

Freshly ground black pepper

2 tablespoons finely minced fresh mint

Pre-prep: Peel oranges (see note); trim top and root from fennel; rinse and dry watercress and spinach, remove leaves from stems, tear spinach; mince mint.

1. Cut each orange horizontally into $\frac{1}{4}$-inch thick slices. Slice the fennel bulb as thin as possible. Place orange slices and fennel in a shallow glass or plastic container.

2. Mix vinegar, orange juice concentrate, oregano and olive oil together and pour over the orange-fennel mixture. Refrigerate at least 30 minutes or up to 4 hours.

3. At serving time, place the watercress and spinach in a salad bowl and drain the juice/dressing from the oranges and fennel onto the greens. Add pepper and mint and toss greens gently. Arrange greens on serving plate; place orange-fennel mixture on top.

Serves 6

Each serving has approximately:

Cals: 98
Total fat: 1.8 g
Sat fat: 0.2 g

Sodium: 37 mg
Chol: None
Fiber: 3 g

Calcium: 110 mg
Carbs: 19 g
Protein: 3 g

note

To peel each orange, slice off the top and bottom horizontally and place flat side down on cutting board. Using a sharp knife, start at the top and slice downward, following the contour of the fruit, removing peel and white membrane completely. Turn orange and repeat, until all the peel has been removed. This way, when you slice the fruit horizontally, you wind up with pretty orange "wheels."

sides: salads

greek green bean salad

This cool summer refresher could just as easily be made with dainty French haricots verts.

1 pound fresh green beans, stems removed

1 teaspoon salt

2 young red onions, about 1½ inches in diameter, sliced very thin

4 fresh tomatoes, cut into ¾-inch cubes

2 small cucumbers, thinly sliced (optional)

2 ounces feta, crumbled

Red Wine Vinaigrette (recipe at right)

¼ cup minced fresh basil and/or mint

Pre-prep: Make vinaigrette. Clean and stem beans; slice onions and cucumbers, if using; cube tomatoes; mince herbs.

1. Bring a large pot of water to boil. Add green beans and salt. Boil just until beans are al dente, testing after 10 minutes (it can take up to 10 minutes longer, depending on the beans); drain and plunge into ice water to stop cooking. Drain and chill until ready to use.

2. Combine green beans, onions, tomatoes and cucumber, if using, in a large salad bowl. Crumble feta into vinaigrette and pour over vegetables, just before serving. Toss lightly, sprinkle with minced herbs and serve.

Serves 4

Each serving has approximately:

Cals: 148	*Sodium: 498 mg*	*Calcium: 148 mg*
Total fat: 6 g	*Chol: 13 mg*	*Carbs: 16 g*
Sat fat: 0.4 g	*Fiber: 5 g*	*Protein: 6 g*

red wine vinaigrette

¼ cup red wine vinegar

¼ cup cream sherry

2 cloves garlic, minced

1 shallot, finely minced

2 teaspoons extra-virgin olive oil

½ teaspoon anchovy paste

½ teaspoon salt or to taste

Freshly ground black pepper

Mix all ingredients together.

variation

Substitute 1 cup of sliced fennel and 2 cups orange sections for tomatoes and cucumbers, and substitute 1 ounce grated Parmesan for feta.

sides: salads

light greek salad

Forget lettuce. Authentic Greek salad is made with tomatoes and cucumbers. We cut the olive oil and feta, without cutting flavor.

3 large ripe tomatoes, cut in bite-size pieces

3 medium cucumbers, peeled, seeded and cut in bite-size pieces

1½ to 2 tablespoons extra-virgin olive oil

¼ cup red wine vinegar

½ teaspoon salt or to taste

2 tablespoons dried oregano, crumbled (preferably Greek)

3 ounces feta cheese

Pre-prep: Cube tomatoes and cucumbers.

Place tomatoes and cucumbers in a large bowl. Add oil, vinegar, salt and oregano and gently toss. Crumble cheese over top. Serve with crusty whole-grain bread to sop up juices.

Serves 6

Each serving has approximately:

Cals: 103	*Sodium: 554 mg*	*Calcium: 87 mg*
Total fat: 8 g	*Chol: 13 mg*	*Carbs: 6 g*
Sat fat: 3 g	*Fiber: 2 g*	*Protein: 3 g*

variation

Add ½ teaspoon dried mint or 2 tablespoons chopped fresh mint, thin-sliced onions and bell peppers. You can even add a tablespoon of good salsa. Make 3 or 4 entree salads by adding ½ cup cubed smoked chicken, turkey or tuna, or 6 medium grilled shrimp per serving.

tip

Red alert: Store tomatoes at room temperature until they get so ripe you have to use them. Storing them in the refrigerator destroys their texture and flavor.

sides: salads

mediterranean salad with roast garlic vinaigrette

What a sensuous blend of flavors: sweet fruit, hot onion, salty feta and tangy vinaigrette. Plus toasted pine nuts for buttery crunch.

1 small head radicchio, thinly sliced

3 cups spinach leaves, rinsed, dried and torn

3 cups red leaf lettuce, rinsed, dried and torn

2 red peppers, roasted and cut into strips (see note)

1 mango, cut into 1-inch chunks, or 2 small nectarines, thinly sliced

1 purple onion, cut in half top to bottom, then thinly sliced vertically

Roast Garlic Vinaigrette (See Page 114)

3 ounces feta cheese, crumbled

12 Nicoise or Kalamata olives (optional)

2 tablespoons toasted pine nuts (see Page 17)

Pre-prep: Make vinaigrette. Roast peppers and slice. Slice radicchio; rinse, dry and tear greens; cube mango and slice onion; toast pine nuts, if using.

Toss radicchio, spinach, red leaf lettuce, pepper strips, mango and onion together with the vinaigrette. Divide and arrange on individual salad plates and garnish with cheese, olives, if using, and pine nuts.

Serves 4

Each serving has approximately:

Cals: 248	*Sodium: 574 mg*	*Calcium: 210 mg*
Total fat: 12 g	*Chol: 19 mg*	*Carbs: 31 g*
Sat fat: 1.1 g	*Fiber: 4 g*	*Protein: 8 g*

note

To roast peppers, cut in half lengthwise and cook in 400°F oven for 25 minutes. When cool enough to handle, peel away skin under cool running water. Discard seeds.

sides: salads

veggies

sensational sides: veggies

George Bush has a point: Even the most dedicated health foodie can eat steamed broccoli only so often. Part of the abiding unpopularity of many vegetables is the prosaic ways they're often prepared. Oven-roasting is a giant step toward boosting flavor, especially for vegetables prone to caramelize, like potatoes, onions and carrots. But it is possible to attain yet a higher plane with recipes such as Sweet Potatoes and Roasted Bananas. They're dashed with a touch of cayenne, and the fruit caramelizes as nicely as the vegetables, adding lushness to a fall staple. When tomatoes are in season, a simple preparation with garlic, herbs, bread crumbs and Parmesan is ambrosial, broiled or grilled. And folding turnips, leeks and horseradish into mashed potatoes both lightens and brightens the soothing comfort food. Maybe George should try Broccoli with Fennel bathed in garlic, Pernod and red pepper flakes. It's not the same old stalk.

easy, delicious swiss chard

If you have never made Swiss chard, it's one of the milder greens and this recipe is just what it says: easy and delicious. Red-stemmed chard has a faint beet flavor.

1 to 2 teaspoons olive oil	**Pepper to taste**
1 large bunch chard, washed	**½ teaspoon sesame oil**
2 to 3 cloves garlic	**Squeeze of lemon juice**
½ teaspoon salt, or to taste	

Pre-prep: Remove stems from chard and cut stems into ¼-inch pieces. Mince garlic. Stack the chard leaves on top of each other and cut into 1x3-inch strips.

1. Place a large skillet over medium heat and add olive oil. When hot, add the chard stems, cover and cook 3 to 4 minutes, stirring a couple of times.

2. Add the chard leaves; use tongs to stir the chard until it reduces some in volume (like spinach). Add the garlic and salt and pepper to taste. Stir again; cover for another 2 minutes, until tender.

3. Drizzle sesame oil and lemon juice over chard; adjust salt and pepper.

Serves 4

Each serving has approximately:

Cals: 33	*Sodium: 444 mg*	*Calcium: 42 mg*
Total fat: 1.8 g	*Chol: None*	*Carbs: 4 g*
Sat fat: 0.2 g	*Fiber: 1 g*	*Protein: 1 g*

variation

Increase the olive oil to 1½ to 2½ teaspoons; omit the sesame oil. Omit the lemon juice; drizzle with balsamic or fruit-flavored vinegar instead.

sides: veggies

broccoli and fennel

Often neglected and frequently mislabled as anise, fennel adds an herblike dimension to plain old broccoli.

2 teaspoons olive oil

1 fennel bulb, thinly sliced

1 tablespoon chopped garlic

¼ teaspoon hot red pepper flakes

½ to 1 cup water

1½ pounds broccoli, trimmed, cut into 1x2-inch florets

Salt to taste

2 tablespoons Pernod (optional)

Pre-prep: Trim top and bottom from fennel and slice; chop garlic; trim broccoli and cut into florets.

1. Heat the oil in a large skillet over medium heat; add the fennel, garlic and pepper flakes. Stir frequently until garlic is golden, then add ½ cup water to the broccoli and salt to taste.

2. Cover with a tight-fitting lid, reduce heat to low and cook for about 10 minutes, or until broccoli is tender. Stir occasionally so florets cook evenly, adding water as necessary. Broccoli should be green and tender when done, and water should be evaporated.

3. Remove skillet from heat; add Pernod, if using. Transfer contents to serving dish.

Serves 4

Each serving has approximately:

Cals: 79	*Sodium: 58 mg*	*Calcium: 98 mg*
Total fat: 2.9 g	*Chol: None*	*Carbs: 12 g*
Sat fat: 0.4 g	*Fiber: 6 g*	*Protein: 6 g*

sides: veggies

cauliflower curry

The wonderful aromatic curry spices transform humble cauliflower into a regal dish — even for people who think they don't like curry.

Butter-flavored cooking spray

1 tablespoon olive oil or butter

½ teaspoon turmeric

½ teaspoon mustard seeds

½ teaspoon cumin seeds

½ teaspoon ground coriander

¼ teaspoon salt

¼ teaspoon cinnamon

¼ teaspoon cayenne

2 cloves garlic, minced

1 tablespoon grated fresh ginger

2 pounds cauliflower, trimmed and broken into florets

¾ cup water

1 (10-ounce) can diced tomatoes and green chiles (see note)

1 cup frozen peas

¼ cup cilantro, basil or mint, or a combination, minced

Nonfat yogurt (optional)

Pre-prep: Mince garlic, ginger and herbs; trim cauliflower and break into florets.

1. Coat a large, heavy skillet with cooking spray, add olive oil or butter. Place over low heat and add the spices. Stir until well mixed and spices are warm, about 2 minutes.

2. Add garlic and ginger; stir for 1 to 2 minutes more; add cauliflower and water. Stir well to coat the cauliflower with spices. Cover tightly, letting cauliflower steam until almost tender, about 8 minutes.

3. Stir in the canned tomatoes and frozen peas; simmer, covered, about 4 minutes longer. Remove from heat and sprinkle with cilantro. Serve with yogurt, if desired.

Serves 4 to 6

Each serving has approximately:

Cals: 96	*Sodium: 298 mg*	*Calcium: 73 mg*
Total fat: 3.4 mg	*Chol: None*	*Carbs: 13 g*
Sat fat: 0.4 mg	*Fiber: 6.5 g*	*Protein: 6 g*

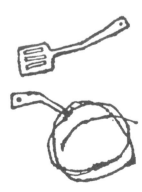

variation

For an entree, mix a second batch of the spices, ginger and garlic, and combine with ½ cup liquid from the tomatoes or water. Cut an 8-ounce block of wild rice flavor or mixed-grain tempeh into ½x¼-inch cubes and add to the spice mixture. Mix well and allow to marinate while cauliflower cooks. Add to cauliflower at the same time as the frozen peas.

note

For a milder dish, use 2 fresh tomatoes or a can of drained, diced tomatoes in place of the canned tomatoes and chiles.

sides: veggies

curried carrots

Fragrant Indian spices, with a touch of sweetness from orange juice, banana and raisins, turn ordinary carrots into an extraordinary curry.

1½ pounds carrots, peeled or scraped, sliced on the diagonal ½-inch thick

2 cups orange juice

Butter-flavored cooking spray

1 tablespoon canola oil or butter

½ teaspoon ground cardamom

½ teaspoon prepared curry powder

1½ teaspoons turmeric

1½ teaspoons mustard seeds

4 whole cloves

1 tablespoon cumin seeds

⅛ teaspoon cayenne pepper (optional)

1 ripe banana, thinly sliced

3 tablespoons golden raisins

1½ tablespoons cornstarch

Pre-prep: Peel or scrape carrots and slice; slice banana.

1. Put carrots and orange juice in a saucepan over medium-high heat; bring to a boil. Reduce heat, cover and simmer for 5 minutes.

2. Meanwhile, coat a large skillet with cooking spray, add canola oil and place over low heat. When oil is warm, add the spices. Heat, stirring, 1 to 2 minutes, then add the carrots and their liquid, the banana and raisins. Cover and simmer over low heat for about 30 minutes, until carrots are tender.

3. Place cornstarch in a small bowl with about ¼ cup of the cooking liquid and mix. When you have a smooth, thin paste, add to carrots and stir well. Heat a few minutes longer to thicken sauce.

Serves 6

Each serving has approximately:

Cals: 156	Sodium: 77 mg	Calcium: 57 mg
Total fat: 3.1 g	Chol: None	Carbs: 32 g
Sat fat: 0.3 g	Fiber: 1 g	Protein: 2 g

tips

The ripe stuff: To quickly ripen a banana, poke several holes in the peel and place in a microwave on High (100% power) for 1 minute.

Currying flavor: Curry powder is a blend of about 20 different spices, and each Indian cook has his or her own formula, which is mixed daily. You can use spice-rack curry, but it never tastes as good as combining the spices yourself.

sides: veggies

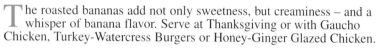

sweet potatoes and roasted bananas

The roasted bananas add not only sweetness, but creaminess – and a whisper of banana flavor. Serve at Thanksgiving or with Gaucho Chicken, Turkey-Watercress Burgers or Honey-Ginger Glazed Chicken.

1½ pounds sweet potatoes, scrubbed

2 medium bananas, peeled and cut in half across

Butter-flavored cooking spray

3 tablespoons orange-flavored liqueur, dark rum or orange juice

½ teaspoon cinnamon

½ teaspoon ground cardamom

¼ teaspoon nutmeg

⅛ to ¼ teaspoon cayenne pepper or to taste (see note)

¼ teaspoon salt or to taste

3 tablespoons brown sugar

1 tablespoon chopped cilantro (optional)

Pre-prep: Scrub sweet potatoes; peel and halve bananas; chop cilantro, if using.

1. Preheat oven to 400° F. Use a sharp fork to pierce the potatoes in several places; place potatoes on oven rack, with a foil-covered baking sheet on the rack below to catch any drips. Bake 50 minutes or until easily pierced by a knife and juices are starting to seep from the holes. Remove from oven.

2. Meanwhile, put bananas in a baking dish coated with cooking spray and bake until bananas are oozing caramel and bottom of dish is golden brown, about 20 minutes. (You can do this in the oven with the sweet potatoes.)

3. Pour the liqueur over the bananas, scrape the brown bits off the bottom of the dish and mash the bananas well.

4. When potatoes are cool enough to handle, remove peel, cut into chunks and transfer to a mixing bowl; add bananas, spices and brown sugar.

5. Mash or beat with electric mixer to desired consistency. (Mixture will be thick.)

6. To serve, coat a 4-ounce ramekin with cooking spray, fill with potatoes and press gently. Turn upside-down over serving plate and, with a firm smack, force potatoes out of ramekin onto the plate. Do this with each serving. Garnish with cilantro, if desired.

Serves 6

Each ¾ cup serving has approximately:

Cals: 201	*Sodium: 160 mg*	*Calcium: 33 mg*
Total fat: 2.9 g	*Chol: None*	*Carbs: 42 g*
Sat fat: 0.5 g	*Fiber: 3 g*	*Protein: 1.5 g*

note

If you make these in advance, go easy on the cayenne. It gets hotter after sitting overnight.

sides: veggies

hot potatoes with roasted corn and poblano peppers

With just a hint of tanginess, these gold- and green-flecked potatoes provide lively counterpoint to Gaucho Chicken or Chile-Rubbed Pan-Fried Chicken.

2 ears corn, in husks, or 1 cup frozen corn, thawed (see note)

2 whole poblano peppers

1½ to 2 pounds baking potatoes, peeled and cut in large pieces

½ cup blended tofu (see Page 17)

½ to 1 cup buttermilk or evaporated fat-free milk

1 tablespoon lime juice

½ teaspoon salt, or to taste and pepper to taste

Pre-prep: Thaw and prepare frozen corn; peel and cut potatoes; blend tofu (see Page 17); juice lime.

1. Preheat oven to 450° F. Dampen corn husks under running water. Place corn and poblano peppers on a rack in the oven and roast for 20 minutes. Cool corn; remove husks and silk. Cut corn from the cobs with serrated knife. Remove and discard the stems from the peppers and dice. Set aside.

2. Cook potatoes in salted, boiling water until tender. Drain; return potatoes to saucepan. Mash roughly; stir in peppers and corn. Stir in tofu and enough buttermilk to reach desired consistency. Finish with lime juice, salt and pepper.

Serves 6

Each serving has approximately:

Cals: 156	*Sodium: 239 mg*	*Calcium: 42 mg*
Total fat: 1 g	*Chol: 1 mg*	*Carbs: 33 g*
Sat fat: 0.3 g	*Fiber: 1 g*	*Protein: 5 g*

variation

For Mashed Potatoes with Goat Cheese and Olives, prepare potatoes as directed, omitting the corn, pepper and lime juice. Instead, stir in 8 seeded and chopped Kalamata olives, 3 to 4 tablespoons goat cheese, 1 tablespoon finely minced fresh thyme and salt and freshly ground pepper to taste.

note

If using frozen corn, sauté 2 minutes in a hot pan coated with olive oil cooking spray until thawed and brown.

sides : veggies

mashed potatoes with turnips, leeks and horseradish

Turnips or cauliflower lighten the texture of these exquisite mashed potatoes; leeks, horseradish and dill make the flavor pop.

Olive oil cooking spray

2 medium turnips, peeled, cut into 1-inch chunks, or 2 cups cauliflower florets (see note)

1 leek, white and light green part only, cut in ¼-inch slices

1 bay leaf

1 (16-ounce) can nonfat chicken broth

2 russet potatoes, about 1½ pounds, peeled and cut into 2-inch pieces

½ cup light and firm silken tofu, blended (see Page 17)

1½ to 2 teaspoons prepared horseradish

½ teaspoon salt or to taste

Freshly ground pepper

Minced fresh dill

Pre-prep: Peel turnips and potatoes and cut into pieces; trim root and green end from leek, hold leek under running water to clean thoroughly, slice; blend tofu (see Page 17); mince dill.

1. Coat a medium saucepan with cooking spray, place over medium heat and add the turnip and leek. Sauté until leeks are soft, about 5 minutes.

2. Add bay leaf and chicken broth to cover vegetables. Bring to a simmer, cover and reduce heat slightly. Simmer until turnips begin to soften, about 5 minutes.

3. Add the potatoes; return to simmer and cook until potatoes and turnips are tender, about 15 more minutes. Uncover for last 5 minutes. Drain well and reserve cooking liquid.

4. Use an electric mixer or potato masher to mash vegetables; don't over-mash. When smooth with a few lumps, add the blended tofu and enough reserved cooking liquid to achieve desired consistency. Stir in horseradish, salt and pepper. Sprinkle with minced dill and serve.

Serves 6

Each serving has approximately:

Cals: 123	*Sodium: 457 mg*	*Calcium: 36 mg*
Total fat: 1.1 g	*Chol: 1 mg*	*Carbs: 25 g*
Sat fat: 0.3 g	*Fiber: 1 g*	*Protein: 5 g*

note

If using cauliflower, omit turnip and skip the 5 minutes of cooking in step No. 2. Place the cauliflower in the pot along with the potatoes, bay leaf and chicken broth to cover. Proceed as directed.

sides: veggies

oven-roasted veggies

With loads of basil and garlic plus caramelized natural sugars from the high heat, these vegetables are anything but ordinary. Roast extra to freeze for Roasted Veggie Pizza or Pasta.

Olive oil cooking spray

1 eggplant, about 1 pound, cut in half

2 large onions, cut in half, papery skin left on

1 red bell pepper, seeded and cut in half

1 poblano pepper, seeded and cut in half

1 to 2 jalapeño chiles, seeded and cut in half (optional)

10 to 12 cloves garlic, papery skins removed

Juice of 2 lemons (about 3 tablespoons)

1 tablespoon olive oil

1 cup chopped fresh basil (divided use)

½ teaspoon salt or to taste

Pre-prep: Cut eggplant, onions, peppers in half; peel garlic; juice lemons; chop basil.

1. Preheat oven to 400° F. Coat a large baking pan with cooking spray; add vegetables, cut side down, and spray again. Bake for about 35 minutes, until vegetables are soft. The eggplant will be soft, but not mushy; the peppers will be brown on the bottom.

2. When cool, remove peel from onions and from peppers, if desired; cut onions, peppers and eggplant into 1-inch cubes.

3. Meanwhile, puree the jalapeño, garlic, lemon juice, olive oil, half the basil and salt in food processor or blender; gently stir into the vegetables. At serving time, stir in all but 2 tablespoons of basil, which are for garnish.

Serves 4

Each serving has approximately:

Cals: 95	*Sodium: 297 mg*	*Calcium: 52 mg*
Total fat: 3.8 g	*Chol: None*	*Carbs: 15 g*
Sat fat: 0.6 g	*Fiber: 3.6 g*	*Protein: 3 g*

variation

For Roasted Veggie Soup, puree the roasted veggies in step No. 2 with 2 cups low-sodium chicken broth, 1 (15½-ounce) can diced tomatoes or Tangy V-8 Juice. (You may have to do this in batches.) Transfer to a large soup kettle. Omit ingredients and preparation in step No. 3. Heat puree to boiling; add 1 cup frozen corn kernels and 4 ounces cooked or smoked turkey or chicken, cut in bite-size pieces, if desired. Reduce heat and simmer only long enough to heat the corn. Season with salt; garnish with freshly chopped cilantro.

tomatoes provençal

This really brings out the flavor of the freshest, most intense seasonal tomatoes; during off months, Roma tomatoes are a good substitute.

4 large, ripe, firm tomatoes, cut in half horizontally (do not peel)

¾ cup fresh French or Italian bread crumbs

2 to 3 cloves garlic, finely minced

6 tablespoons finely minced basil or other fresh herb

3 tablespoons grated Parmesan

2 tablespoons finely chopped black olives

⅛ teaspoon salt, or to taste, and pepper to taste

Olive oil cooking spray

Pre-prep: Halve tomatoes; mince garlic, herbs; grate cheese; chop olives.

1. With a spoon (a grapefruit spoon works best), remove and discard seeds and soft center of each tomato half.

2. Combine bread crumbs, garlic, herbs, cheese and olives. Season with salt and pepper. Spoon about 2 tablespoons filling into each tomato half; spray with cooking spray. Place tomatoes under broiler until filling is golden, about 5 minutes. You can also cook these tomatoes on the grill for a wonderful smoky dimension.

Serves 4

Each serving has approximately:

Cals: 91	*Sodium: 334 mg*	*Calcium: 88 mg*
Total fat: 2.8 g	*Chol: 3 mg*	*Carbs: 14 g*
Sat fat: 1 g	*Fiber: 2 g*	*Protein: 4 g*

variation

Use fresh mint and feta cheese, or use parsley and Roquefort cheese in place of the basil and Parmesan.

tip

Easy bread crumbs: Anytime you have some good bread left over, throw it in the food processor with some garlic for easy homemade bread crumbs. Freeze in a zip-top bag to use with recipes such as Tomatoes Provençal or to add a special finish to other dishes.

sides: veggies

garlicky oven-roasted potatoes

These potatoes and the golden garlic cloves that roast with them make a lovely side dish. Save any leftovers to top a main-dish salad.

Olive oil cooking spray
½ teaspoon seasoned salt
Pepper

1 pound small, red new potatoes, washed
8 cloves garlic

Pre-prep: Peel garlic cloves; wash potatoes.

Fire up the oven to 400° F. Coat a baking dish large enough to hold the potatoes in a single layer with cooking spray. Sprinkle the bottom with ¹/₂ teaspoon seasoned salt and pepper; add potatoes. Shake the dish gently so the potatoes roll around and pick up the seasoning. Bake for 20 minutes. Add garlic cloves. Bake for about 30 more minutes, until potatoes are easily pierced with a knife and garlic is golden.

Serves 4

Each serving has approximately:

Cals: 175   *Sodium: 203 mg*   *Calcium: 26 mg*
Total fat: 0.2 g   *Chol: None*   *Carbs: 41 g*
Sat fat: None   *Fiber: <1 g*   *Protein: 4 g*

spiced sweet potato rounds

So simple to make and so tasty. A bit of salt will also make them taste sweeter.

Butter-flavor cooking spray
Cinnamon
Cardamom

Ground clove
Ground ginger
2 medium sweet potatoes

Pre-prep: Scrub sweet potatoes, leaving the skins on. Cut into ³/₄-inch thick rounds.

Preheat oven to 400° F. Coat a shallow baking dish with cooking spray; sprinkle a generous layer of cinnamon, cardamom, ground clove and ground ginger on the bottom. Add sweet potatoes. Now sprinkle another generous layer of the spices on the top sides; spray with cooking spray, and bake for 25 minutes. Cover with aluminum foil and return to oven for 10 minutes more, until rounds are easily pierced with a fork.

Serves 4

Each serving has approximately:

Cals: 142   *Sodium: 17 mg*   *Calcium: 35 mg*
Total fat: 0.4 g   *Chol: None*   *Carbs: 33 g*
Sat fat: None   *Fiber: <1 g*   *Protein: 2 g*

sides :: veggies

grains & quick breads

sensational sides

sensational sides: grains and quick breads

The greatest challenge with grains is shedding their health-food image. And, in truth, you can't entirely. So we give grains a lighter touch than other plant foods. We take a familiar dish like tabbouleh and give it a new face with arugula or watercress, using a generations-old Lebanese method to bring out the flavors. We use tofu — yes, here it is again — to produce moist, sumptuous muffins that exceed all expectations. Then we weave in chocolate chunks and watch resistance melt. Southwest Corn Pudding laced with chiles, tomatoes, cilantro and cheese, does such an amazing number with soy grits — a corn grits knockoff — that guests not only go back for seconds. They want thirds. If all this stretches the outer limits of your pioneering spirit, take heart: Two of the best, simplest ways to eat grains still are breakfast cereals and breads, especially rustic breads. But dare to try one, just one, of these recipes; you won't be disappointed.

bulgur salad with sun-dried tomatoes, basil and almonds

Bulgur, so friendly in tabbouleh, gets star treatment here with more flavors of the Middle East — at its best warm or room temperature.

1½ cups orange juice

1 cup bulgur wheat

¼ cup water

6 to 8 sun-dried tomato pieces

Olive oil cooking spray

1 large onion, finely chopped

2 cloves garlic, finely minced

2 cups diced mushrooms

2 tablespoons tomato paste

½ cup fresh basil and mint leaves, minced

¼ cup chopped toasted almonds (see Page 17)

1 teaspoon salt

Black pepper to taste

1 teaspoon extra-virgin olive oil or basil-flavored olive oil

2 tomatoes, diced

Pre-prep: Chop onion; mince garlic, basil and mint; dice mushrooms and tomatoes. Toast almonds (see Page 17) and chop.

1. Heat orange juice to boiling, pour over bulgur in a large bowl and allow to stand, covered, for about 1 hour. Liquid should be absorbed and wheat should be tender. Note: If there's a little juice left, but the bulgur is tender, just pour the juice off. If there's juice left and the bulgur isn't tender, pop the bowl in the microwave and heat on Medium (50% power) until the liquid is absorbed.

2. Heat ¼ cup water to boiling and pour over dried tomatoes for at least 10 minutes to soften; drain and finely dice tomatoes.

3. Spray a skillet with cooking spray and place over medium heat. Sauté onion and garlic until translucent; add mushrooms, stir and cook about 3 minutes longer. (Mushrooms will still be firm.) Remove from heat, stir in tomato paste and dried tomatoes; stir into bulgur and allow to cool.

4. Just before serving, gently stir in herbs, almonds, salt, pepper, oil and diced tomato. Serve as a side dish with grilled meat or seafood or as part of a main-dish salad.

Serves 6

Each ¾ cup serving has approximately:

Cals: 187	*Sodium: 415 mg*	*Calcium: 59 mg*
Total fat: 4.7 g	*Chol: None*	*Carbs: 33 g*
Sat fat: 0.4 g	*Fiber: 6 g*	*Protein: 7 g*

sides: grains & breads

walnut-mint bulgur

Serve this on your own main-dish salads or with grilled meats such as pork or lamb.

1½ cups apple juice or water

½ teaspoon salt

1 cup bulgur wheat

1 large shallot, finely minced

2 tablespoons minced mint

2 teaspoons walnut oil or extra-virgin olive oil

2 tablespoons chopped walnuts, toasted (see Page 17)

Freshly ground black pepper

Pre-prep: Mince shallot and mint; chop and toast walnuts (see Page 17).

1. Bring juice or water and salt to a boil in a small saucepan. Stir in bulgur, reduce heat; cover and cook over low heat until liquid is absorbed, about 10 to 12 minutes.

2. Transfer bulgur to a serving bowl, fluff with a fork and cool completely.

3. Stir in shallot, mint, oil and toasted walnuts. Season to taste with salt and pepper.

Serves 4

Each serving has approximately:

Cals: 197

Total fat: 4.2 g

Sat fat: 0.5 g

Sodium: 303 mg

Chol: None

Fiber: 6.6 g

Calcium: 21 mg

Carbs: 37 g

Protein: 5 g

not tabbouleh

It's Not Tabbouleh because of the addition of tea and mixed greens, but it's made using a generations-old Lebanese family technique.

½ cup bulgur wheat

3 tablespoons strong tea (see note)

3 medium tomatoes, seeded and diced

1 tablespoon olive oil

3 to 4 cloves garlic, finely minced

1 teaspoon salt

Freshly ground pepper

1½ cups, minced, any combination of fresh greens, such as arugula, mint, watercress or parsley

6 green onions, including tops, chopped

1 medium cucumber, peeled, seeded and diced

¼ cup fresh lemon juice

Pre-prep: Make tea (see note). Seed and dice tomatoes; mince garlic and greens; chop onions; peel, seed and dice cucumber; juice lemons.

1. Place bulgur in a bowl in the sink. Fill with water and allow water to run slowly so it overflows the bowl but doesn't carry the bulgur with it. When runoff water is clear, allow the bulgur to soak for about 10 minutes.

2. Drain well; stir in the tea and refrigerate several hours or overnight.

3. Place tomatoes in a small bowl with olive oil, garlic, salt and pepper; mix to blend and allow to marinate about 30 minutes.

4. Gently stir tomatoes and marinade into bulgur, along with the greens, onions, cucumber and lemon juice. Adjust seasonings to taste.

Serves 4

Each serving has approximately:

Cals: 133	*Sodium: 594 mg*	*Calcium: 94 mg*
Total fat: 4 g	*Chol: None*	*Carbs: 22 g*
Sat fat: 0.6 g	*Fiber: 5 g*	*Protein: 4 g*

note

To make strong tea, bring ½ cup water to boiling, add 1 tea bag and allow to stand for 5 minutes; remove bag before using.

sides: grains & breads

sides: Grains & breads

tri-grain pilaf with roast garlic vinaigrette

Here's a smashing introduction to some of the more exotic whole grains.

Olive oil cooking spray

1 to 2 bell peppers, seeded and cut in half

3 cups water

1 teaspoon salt

¼ cup millet

½ cup quinoa, rinsed

½ cup bulgur wheat

1 cup frozen green peas, thawed

½ cup currants or raisins, soaked for 10 minutes in water and drained

2 tablespoons chopped fresh mint

2 tablespoons chopped fresh basil

Roast Garlic Vinaigrette (recipe at right)

6 red lettuce leaves

Assorted seasonal fruits, or roasted vegetables, sliced

Pre-prep: Seed and halve peppers; rinse quinoa; thaw green peas; soak and drain currants; chop herbs; cut roasted vegetables, if using.

1. Preheat oven to 400° F. Coat a pie pan with cooking spray and place peppers in pan, skin-side down; spray with cooking spray and place in oven for 25 minutes. (Note: You can roast garlic for the dressing and roast the vegetables, if using, at the same time.)

2. Meanwhile, bring water and salt to a boil in a medium saucepan. Add millet, reduce heat to simmer; cover, and cook 5 minutes. Add quinoa and bulgur; cover, and continue cooking for 20 minutes or until water is absorbed. Remove lid, fluff grain with fork and allow to cool.

3. When roasted peppers are cool enough to handle, gently peel away skin under running water. Cut into lengthwise slices. Combine cooked grains, peas, currants, pepper slices and fresh herbs. To serve, pack pilaf into a 4-ounce custard cup or souffle dish. Invert on a lettuce leaf and surround with fresh fruit or roasted veggies. Repeat for each serving.

Serves 6

Each serving has approximately:

Cals: 258	*Sodium: 803 mg*	*Calcium: 66 mg*
Total fat: 4 g	*Chol: None*	*Carbs: 49 g*
Sat fat: 0.5 g	*Fiber: 7.5 g*	*Protein: 8 g*

roast garlic vinaigrette

1 head garlic

1 to 2 shallots, peeled and roughly chopped

⅓ cup balsamic vinegar

1 tablespoon Dijon mustard (see note)

2 tablespoons cream sherry

1 tablespoon olive oil

1 teaspoon salt or to taste

Pre-prep: Peel and chop shallots.

Note: Omit the mustard for the Mediterranean Salad on Page 96.

1. Preheat oven to 400° F. Cut garlic head in half, horizontally. Keeping halves together, place root-side-down on a piece of foil; bring sides of foil up and twist closed. Place in small baking dish and bake for about 50 minutes.

2. Remove from foil to cool, then squeeze baked garlic from the top and bottom sections into bowl of a small food processor or blender. Add shallots and puree. Add remaining ingredients and mix well.

savory corn griddle cakes

Brighten brunch or supper with these springy, colorful griddle cakes; serve with Spicy Carribean Salsa and a dollop of yogurt. Or Roasted Red Pepper Cream.

¾ cup unbleached flour

½ cup cornmeal

1 teaspoon baking soda

½ teaspoon salt

1 tablespoon sugar

1 egg, slightly beaten

1¼ cups buttermilk

1 tablespoon oil

¾ cup frozen corn, thawed

1 red jalapeño chile, seeds and membrane removed, finely minced

2 tablespoons chopped cilantro (optional)

Nonstick cooking spray

Pre-prep: Thaw corn; mince jalapeño chile and cilantro, if using.

1. Combine flour, cornmeal, baking soda, salt and sugar in a mixing bowl.

2. In another small bowl, whisk the egg, buttermilk and oil together; stir into the flour mixture along with the corn, jalapeño chile and cilantro, if using.

3. Coat a griddle or heavy skillet with cooking spray and place over moderately high heat. For each griddle cake, pour about ¼ cup batter onto the hot griddle, forming a 4- to 5-inch round.

4. Turn griddle cakes when bubbles form on the top and the bottoms are golden. Continue to cook on second side until cooked through, another 3 or 4 minutes. Keep cakes covered in warm oven on lowest setting until ready to serve (up to 15 minutes).

Serves 4

Each serving has approximately:

Cals: 258	*Sodium: 705 mg*	*Calcium: 102 mg*
Total fat: 6 g	*Chol: 57 mg*	*Carbs: 43 g*
Sat fat: 1.2 g	*Fiber: 3 g*	*Protein: 9 g*

sides: grains & breads

southwest corn pudding

Like a fritatta-cheese grits hybrid, this fabulous brunch dish is difficult to describe, easy to savor. Soy grits are just like their Southern cousin, except for all those benefits you're not supposed to think about.

Nonstick cooking spray

1 tablespoon canola oil

¾ cup nonfat milk

½ cup water

¾ cup soy or corn grits

½ teaspoon garlic salt

3 ounces low-fat Cheddar cheese or part skim mozzarella, shredded

3 medium eggs or ¾ cup egg substitute

1 (10-ounce) can diced tomatoes and chiles

¾ cup frozen corn, thawed

2 tablespoons green onions, sliced

1½ teaspoons ground cumin

¼ cup cilantro, chopped (divided use)

Roasted Red Pepper Cream (see Page 36)

Pre-prep: Thaw corn. Slice green onions; chop cilantro.

1. Preheat oven to 350° F. Coat a shallow 8- or 9-inch baking pan with cooking spray. Place oil, milk and water in a medium saucepan over medium-high heat and bring to boiling. Gradually stir in grits and garlic salt with a wire whisk to prevent lumping.

2. Reduce heat to low, stirring occasionally until grits have absorbed the liquid and are dry, about 10 to 12 minutes. (Or, if using corn grits, cover and simmer 4 to 5 minutes.) Remove from heat; stir in the cheese.

3. In a large bowl, beat eggs with wire whisk; add tomatoes and chilies, corn, green onions and cumin. Slowly stir cooked grits into egg mixture; mix well, then stir in 2 tablespoons chopped cilantro.

4. Pour into prepared baking dish and bake 45 minutes, until knife inserted in center comes out clean. Cut squares of corn pudding and serve warm with Roasted Red Pepper Cream and cilantro garnish.

Serves 4 to 6

Each serving has approximately:

Cals: 263
Total fat: 11.7 g
Sat fat: 3.6 g

Sodium: 630 mg
Chol: 140 mg
Fiber: 5 g

Calcium: 279 mg
Carbs: 21 g
Protein: 21 g

note

This recipe can easily be doubled using a 10x13-inch baking dish. It also reheats very well so you can make it ahead.

sides: grains & breads

pear spice muffins

These elegantly flavored muffins get some heft from whole wheat flour, but tofu and fruit keep them light.

Nonstick cooking spray

2 large pears, peeled, cored, finely diced (about 2 cups)

⅓ cup brown sugar

½ cup light and firm silken tofu, blended (see Page 17)

1 tablespoon canola oil

1 egg

1 teaspoon vanilla

1¼ teaspoons cinnamon

½ teaspoon nutmeg

⅛ teaspoon allspice

1 cup whole wheat flour

½ teaspoon salt

1 teaspoon baking soda

⅛ cup golden raisins

Pre-prep: Peel, core and dice pears; blend tofu.

1. Preheat oven to 375° F. Coat a muffin tin with cooking spray; set aside. In a large mixing bowl, mix pears with sugar. Add tofu, oil, egg and vanilla, stirring to blend.

2. Add remaining ingredients, and stir quickly just until mixed, taking care to not overmix or muffins will be tough. Lumps are good.

3. Divide batter among prepared muffin cups. Bake until tester inserted in the center of a muffin comes out clean, about 20 minutes.

Makes 10

Each muffin has approximately:

Cals: 124
Total fat: 2.4 g
Sat fat: 0.3 g

Sodium: 253 mg
Chol: 21 mg
Fiber: 2.6 g

Calcium: 23 mg
Carbs: 25 g
Protein: 3 g

tip

Keep it cool: Whole-grain flours contain more oil than refined flours and so are more vulnerable to rancidity. Store them in the freezer if they will not be used within 2 months.

sides: grains & breads

pumpkin clove muffins

Get a great blast of fall flavors with these muffins. Whole-wheat flour makes them a little health-foodie, but you can always tart them up with Streusel Topping.

Nonstick cooking spray

1 teaspoon canola oil

1 whole egg

2 egg whites

1¼ cups canned pumpkin

⅓ cup orange juice

¾ cup sugar

¼ cup golden raisins

¾ cup whole wheat flour

1 cup unbleached flour

½ teaspoon nutmeg

½ teaspoon cinnamon

½ teaspoon cloves

½ teaspoon ginger

1 teaspoon baking soda

¼ teaspoon baking powder

¼ teaspoon salt

Streusel Topping
(optional, recipe at right)

Pre-prep: Separate 2 eggs and reserve yolks for another use. Make Streusel Topping, if using.

1. Preheat oven to 375° F. Coat a 12-cup muffin tin with cooking spray. In a medium mixing bowl, blend together oil, egg, egg whites, pumpkin, orange juice, sugar and raisins.

2. In a large mixing bowl, blend remaining ingredients except topping. Add the moist ingredients to the dry, blending just until mixed. Resist the urge to overmix. Lumps really are good.

3. Fill each muffin cup about three-fourths full and sprinkle with Streusel Topping, if using. Bake for 25 minutes, or until tester comes out clean. Cool in the pan for 15 minutes, remove muffins and place on cooling rack.

Makes 10

Each muffin has approximately:

Cals: 179
Total fat: 1.4 g
Sat fat: 0.3 g

Sodium: 265 mg
Chol: 21 mg
Fiber: 2 g

Calcium: 28 mg
Carbs: 38 g
Protein: 5 g

streusel topping

4 tablespoons flour

4 tablespoons brown sugar

6 tablespoons oats (quick or regular)

½ teaspoon cinnamon

½ teaspoon nutmeg

1½ tablespoons soft butter

Mix together all ingredients until crumbly.

cranberry–almond muffins

It's hard to believe these tenderest of muffins are so nutritious (thanks to sneaky tofu *and* soy flour). And the chocolate-chip ones are even better, if that's possible.

Nonstick cooking spray

Peel of 1 orange

½ cup sugar

2 eggs, lightly beaten

2 tablespoons canola oil

½ cup light and firm silken tofu, blended (see Page 17)

1¼ cups unbleached all purpose flour

¼ cup soy flour (see note)

1 teaspoon baking powder

¼ teaspoon baking soda

¼ teaspoon salt

⅓ cup unblanched almonds, finely chopped

½ cup dried cranberries, coarsely chopped

Pre-prep: Remove orange peel with a vegetable peeler, or grate. Blend tofu (see Page 17). Chop almonds and cranberries.

1. Preheat oven to 375° F. Coat muffin tin with cooking spray; set aside. Put orange peel and sugar in the bowl of a small food processor and process 1 to 2 minutes until the sugar is orange colored. Or, mince or grate orange peel and mix with sugar. Turn into a mixing bowl with the eggs, oil and tofu. Beat with a wire whisk until smooth.

2. Place flours, baking powder, soda and salt in mixing bowl, stir well. Add the almonds and cranberries, then pour the liquid ingredients over dry ingredients and mix quickly just until blended; batter will be lumpy. Resist the urge to overmix or muffins will be tough.

3. Fill muffin cups about three-fourths full. Bake 15 minutes, until golden and springy to the touch.

Makes 12

Each muffin has approximately:

Cals: 166 *Sodium: 126 mg* *Calcium: 40 mg*
Total fat: 5.7 g *Chol: 35 mg* *Carbs: 25 g*
Sat fat: 0.7 g *Fiber: 1 g* *Protein: 4 g*

variation

For Chocolate Chip Muffins, substitute 3 ounces mini-chocolate chips for the dried cranberries. Omit almonds, if desired.

note

Soy flour makes the muffins moist and tender. If you don't have soy flour, you can substitute all-purpose flour and bake the muffins 5 minutes longer, but they won't be quite as good.

sides: grains & breads

fruited couscous

Though often mistaken for a grain, couscous is actually itty-bitty pasta. This easy version can top a main-dish salad, chicken or pork.

1½ cups apple juice or chicken broth

⅓ cup dried fruit, such as golden raisins, prunes or cranberries

1 cup whole wheat couscous

¼ teaspoon allspice

½ teaspoon cinnamon

Salt to taste

Bring apple juice or chicken broth to boiling. Add the fruit, couscous, allspice and cinnamon. Cover, turn off heat and let stand about 10 minutes. Alternately, microwave for 1 to 2 minutes on Low (30% power) until the liquid is absorbed. Fluff with a fork, add salt to taste and serve.

Serves 7

Each ⅓ cup serving has approximately

Cals: 152
Total fat: 0.1 g
Sat fat: None

Sodium: 8 mg
Chol: None
Fiber: 3 g

Calcium: 10 mg
Carbs: 37 g
Protein: 3 g

quick quinoa

Quinoa is one of those lesser-known alternative grains. With a basic recipe like this, you can add onions, garlic, mushrooms, herbs – just about anything you would add to rice to perk up the flavor.

2 cups salted water, vegetable, or chicken broth

1 cup quinoa

Salt to taste

In a small saucepan, heat liquid to boiling; add quinoa. Reduce heat, cover and simmer 15 minutes. Remove lid, fluff with a fork, add salt to taste and serve.

Serves 4

Each serving has approximately:

Cals: 159
Total fat: 2.5 g
Sat fat: 0.3 g

Sodium: 303 mg
Chol: None
Fiber: 2.5 g

Calcium: 28 mg
Carbs: 29 g
Protein: 6 g

sides: grains & breads

sweet endings

desserts

sweet endings

S trictly speaking, you could omit desserts entirely from plant-centered cuisine, so little do they bring to the table. But by now it should be clear that we're intent on nourishing the spirit — and taste buds — as well as the body. And for those who love food, dessert is nothing less than the consummation of a fine meal. Roquefort-Apple Custard and tequila-laced Margarita Sherbet are the most grown-up, sophisticated finishes. Lemon Cloud with Berry Sauce crosses a tart lemon meringue pie with a floating island. Orange-Raspberry Dream Ripple is as voluptuous as homemade ice cream. Each dessert in its way satisfies a craving, whether for chocolate or for cheesecake. We manage to weave in at least fruit, and, once again, tofu — not because it's good for you but because it is an amazing ingredient. When you finish with these sweet endings, all that will be left is to put out the light.

apple clafouti

Inspired by the rich French dessert, this version uses fewer eggs and less butter, yet achieves the same voluptuous results.

2 tablespoons butter

3 Golden Delicious apples, peeled, cored and sliced ¼-inch thick

¼ cup brandy

⅔ cup sugar (divided use)

¼ teaspoon cinnamon

2 whole eggs

1 egg white

¼ cup light and firm silken tofu, blended (see Page 17)

½ cup fat-free milk

1 teaspoon vanilla

⅓ cup all-purpose flour

Butter-flavored cooking spray

Nutmeg

Pre-prep: Peel and slice apples; prepare egg white; blend tofu.

1. Heat butter in large skillet over medium-high heat; add apples. Cook until golden, about 8 minutes, stirring perhaps once. Pour in brandy, ⅓ cup sugar and cinnamon; remove from heat and allow apples to macerate for 30 minutes. Drain apples, reserving liquid.

2. Preheat oven to 350° F. In a mixing bowl, whisk eggs, egg white, tofu, milk, liquid from apples, vanilla and remaining ⅓ cup sugar.

3. Place flour in a large bowl; make a well in the center and slowly pour in the egg mixture, whisking until smooth.

4. Spray a pie or tart pan with cooking spray. Arrange apple slices in pan and cover with batter. Sprinkle with nutmeg and bake for 50 minutes, until golden brown and firm.

5. Cool slightly; slice into wedges and serve warm with low-fat frozen yogurt or low-fat ice cream, if desired.

Serves 6

Each serving has approximately:

Cals: 266
Total fat: 6.4 g
Sat fat: 3 g

Sodium: 86 mg
Chol: 82 mg
Fiber: 2 g

Calcium: 45 mg
Carbs: 42 g
Protein: 5 g

sweet endings

pear and apple pound cake

Pear-apple layers deepen the richness of this cinnamon-spiked dessert, made tender and moist from oft-maligned tofu.

2 Granny Smith apples, peeled, cored and thinly sliced

3 ripe, firm pears, peeled, cored and thinly sliced

2 cups sugar (divided use)

3 teaspoons cinnamon (divided use)

Nonstick cooking spray

3 cups flour

3 teaspoons baking powder

1 teaspoon salt

¾ cup light and firm silken tofu, blended (see Page 17)

¼ cup canola oil

4 eggs

2½ teaspoons vanilla

¼ cup orange juice

Pre-prep: Peel apples and pears, core and slice; blend tofu.

1. Mix apples and pears with ½ cup sugar and 2 teaspoons cinnamon, allow to sit for about 20 minutes. Pour off the juice and reserve.

2. Preheat oven to 350° F. Coat Bundt or tube pan with cooking spray. In a mixing bowl, combine flour, baking powder, salt, tofu, oil, eggs, remaining sugar, vanilla and orange juice. Beat by hand or on medium speed with mixer until smooth, about 3 to 4 minutes.

3. Pour half the batter into the prepared pan; add half the apple-pear mixture. Pour in the remaining batter and top with remaining apples and pears.

4. Bake 1¼ to 1½ hours, until a toothpick inserted in the center comes out clean.

5. Remove cake from oven and cool in pan for 20 minutes. Turn out onto a cooling rack.

6. Meanwhile, mix 1 teaspoon cinnamon and reserved apple-pear juice together; warm in the microwave. Drizzle over finished cake.

Serves 18

Each serving has approximately:

Cals: 250	*Sodium: 206 mg*	*Calcium: 72 mg*
Total fat: 4.6 g	*Chol: 47 mg*	*Carbs: 47 g*
Sat fat: 0.6 g	*Fiber: 2 g*	*Protein: 4 g*

roquefort-apple custard

S erved warm, this makes a wonderful dessert or a cheese course with fresh fruit. At room temperature, it's an elegant appetizer with warm French bread.

Butter-flavored cooking spray

1 tablespoon butter

2 medium Granny Smith apples, peeled, cored and sliced ⅛-inch thick

Pinch nutmeg

5 tablespoons sugar (divided use)

1 tablespoon brandy

2 tablespoons (1 to 2 ounces) Roquefort cheese, crumbled

2 eggs

½ cup light and firm silken tofu, blended (see Page 17)

2½ cups evaporated fat-free milk

¾ teaspoon vanilla

Pre-prep: Peel, core and slice apples; blend tofu.

1. Preheat oven to 300° F. Coat a 10-inch tart dish with cooking spray; set aside. Melt butter in a heavy sauté pan over medium heat; add apple slices, stirring to coat. Sprinkle with nutmeg and 1 tablespoon sugar. Cook, stirring only occasionally, until apples begin to turn golden, about 8 minutes. Just before removing from heat, add brandy, stirring to evaporate.

2. Place apple slices in bottom of prepared dish. Crumble cheese over top.

3. In a bowl, whisk the eggs, tofu, remaining sugar, milk and vanilla until well blended. Pour into apples and cheese.

4. Bake until custard is set, about 40 minutes. A knife should come out clean when inserted in the center. Serve warm or at room temperature.

Serves 8

Each serving has approximately:

Cals: 174	*Sodium: 230 mg*	*Calcium: 281 mg*
Total fat: 4.8 g	*Chol: 65 mg*	*Carbs: 22 g*
Sat fat: 2.5 g	*Fiber: <1 g*	*Protein: 10 g*

sweet endings

bananas diablo

S picy, sweet, hot and cool, this dessert bedevils the senses — in the best way.

Butter-flavored cooking spray

1 teaspoon butter

½ jalapeño chile, seeded and finely minced

2 teaspoons grated fresh ginger

⅓ cup dark brown sugar

2 tablespoons ginger liqueur or orange liqueur

3 ripe but firm bananas, sliced in half lengthwise, then crosswise

2 cups nonfat vanilla frozen yogurt or low-fat ice cream

Pre-prep: Mince chile; grate ginger; slice bananas.

1. Coat a medium skillet with cooking spray. Place over moderate heat and melt butter. Add the chile and ginger; sauté for about 1 minute.

2. Add the brown sugar, stirring until it melts; swirl in the liqueur.

3. Gently lay bananas in sauce, turning once or twice to coat; warm just long enough to heat through.

4. Serve 3 pieces of banana over nonfat vanilla frozen yogurt or low-fat ice cream.

Serves 4

Each serving has approximately:

Cals: 266   *Sodium: 83 mg*   *Calcium: 106 mg*
Total fat: 1.4 g   *Chol: 3 mg*   *Carbs: 59 g*
Sat fat: 0.8 g   *Fiber: 2 g*   *Protein: 5 g*

tip

A-peeling ginger: Fresh ginger needn't be peeled before using — just rinse with water and grate or mince.

banana-cinnamon bread pudding

Who can resist really good bread pudding? Go ahead and double this light, elegant recipe; it freezes well.

2 eggs

1 cup fat-free milk

¼ cup plus 2 tablespoons brown sugar (divided use)

1 cup banana-flavored nonfat yogurt

½ teaspoon nutmeg

1 teaspoon cinnamon

8 ounces mixed-grain bread, cut into ½-inch cubes

Butter-flavored cooking spray

4 large ripe bananas, sliced (divided use)

¼ cup raisins

½ cup maple syrup

Pre-prep: Cube bread and slice 2 of the bananas into coins.

1. In a large bowl, mix together eggs, milk, ¼ cup brown sugar, yogurt, nutmeg and cinnamon. Add bread; mix well and refrigerate at least 15 minutes.

2. Preheat oven to 325° F. Coat an 8- or 9-inch baking dish with cooking spray.

3. Stir the banana coins and the raisins into the custard. Pour all ingredients into prepared pan and sprinkle top with 2 tablespoons brown sugar. Bake for about 45 minutes, until brown and firm.

4. Slice remaining bananas into coins. Mix with maple syrup and heat gently. Drizzle over each serving.

Serves 8

Each serving has approximately:

Cals: 273	Sodium: 226 mg	Calcium: 149 mg
Total fat: 2.5 g	Chol: 54 mg	Carbs: 58 g
Sat fat: 0.8 g	Fiber: 2.5 g	Protein: 7 g

amaretto creme

1 (12.3-ounce) package light and firm silken tofu

3 tablespoons sugar

2 tablespoons melted butter

¼ cup Amaretto liqueur

1. Place the tofu in the bowl of a food processor and blend until smooth and creamy.

2. Add remaining ingredients and process till mixed.

3. Transfer to a microwave-proof bowl and gently heat on low power for 1 to 2 minutes, until warm. Ladle over bread pudding as an alternative sauce. Serves 8.

sweetendings

lemon cloud with blueberry sauce

This delicate dessert combines the best of lemon meringue pie and a floating island. For more decadence, serve with shortbread cookies.

Nonstick cooking spray

⅔ plus ¼ cup sugar (divided use)

⅓ cup unbleached flour

1 tablespoon grated orange or lemon peel

7 tablespoons fresh lemon juice (about 3½ small lemons)

2 tablespoons melted butter

2 whole eggs, room temperature

1½ cups buttermilk

2 egg whites, room temperature

Blueberry Sauce (recipe at right)

Pre-prep: Make Blueberry Sauce. Grate orange or lemon peel; juice lemons; melt butter; separate 1 egg (reserving the yolk and white); bring these, an additional egg and the 2 egg whites to room temperature.

1. Position rack in center of oven and preheat to 350º F. Coat a 6- to 8-cup glass souffle mold or baking pan with cooking spray.

2. Blend ⅔ cup sugar and flour in large bowl; add orange peel, lemon juice, melted butter, 1 whole egg and 1 egg yolk (reserve white). Stir in buttermilk.

3. In another clean, dry bowl, combine reserved white with egg whites (3 total) and beat until soft peaks form; gradually add ¼ cup sugar until stiff peaks form.

4. Fold most of the whites into buttermilk mixture; pour into prepared mold, leaving some stiff egg whites in mounds on top.

5. Place mold in large pan with enough hot water to come halfway up the side of the mold. Bake until top is golden brown, about 1 hour.

6. Carefully remove dish from water bath and let cool for at least 15 minutes before serving with Blueberry Sauce.

Serves 6

Each serving has approximately:

Cals: 296   *Sodium: 151 mg*   *Calcium: 88 mg*
Total fat: 6.6 g   *Chol: 84 mg*   *Carbs: 52 g*
Sat fat: 3.4 g   *Fiber: 1 g*   *Protein: 6 g*

blueberry sauce

¼ cup apricot or peach preserves

2 tablespoons cognac

1 cup fresh or frozen blueberries

Dash of nutmeg

1. Mix preserves and cognac together; warm over low heat or in the microwave on Medium (50% power), adding 1 tablespoon of water, if necessary, to reach saucelike consistency.

2. Add blueberries and gently heat until warm. Sprinkle with nutmeg just before serving.

sweet endings

blackberry–rhubarb cobbler

The tang of rhubarb mingles with the sweetness of berries under a crisp cookielike topping to make this cobbler sensational. Flavoring the sugar adds a delicate citrus dimension.

Peel of 1 orange	1 (16-ounce) bag frozen rhubarb
⅓ cup sugar	1 tablespoon flour
1 (16-ounce) bag frozen blackberries	Cobbler Topping (recipe at left)

Pre-prep: Make topping. Remove peel of orange with a vegetable peeler or grate orange peel.

1. Preheat oven to 350° F. Place the orange peel in a food processor or blender with the sugar. Keep motor running until sugar turns orange and peel is no longer visible. Or, grate the peel and stir it into the sugar by hand.

2. Spread blackberries and rhubarb in the bottom of a 9x13-inch glass baking dish; sprinkle with flavored sugar and flour.

3. Evenly "blob" topping onto filling and, with fingers, spread over all the fruit. (Be patient, as the very moist topping sticks to your fingers. Some fruit will show through.)

4. Bake for 60 to 70 minutes, until top is dark golden brown and has a dull sound when thumped.

Serves 8

Each serving has approximately:

Cals: 280	*Sodium: 90 mg*	*Calcium: 68 mg*
Total fat: 7.7 g	*Chol: 35 mg*	*Carbs: 51 g*
Sat Fat: 2.4 g	*Fiber: 4 g*	*Protein: 4 g*

cobbler topping

1 cup flour

¾ cup sugar

1 teaspoon baking powder

1 egg

2 tablespoons canola oil

2 tablespoons melted, cooled butter

1. Combine flour, sugar and baking powder in a medium bowl; stir well.

2. In a separate bowl, mix egg, canola oil and butter.

3. Pour the liquid into flour mixture, stirring with a fork until well blended.

sweet endings

orange-raspberry dream ripple

Richer tasting than it ought to be, this frozen dessert has the subtle evaporated-milk tang that flavors many home-cranked ice creams, but almost none of the fat.

1 cup evaporated fat-free milk, chilled

1 (12.3-ounce) package light and extra-firm silken tofu, drained

⅓ cup plus 3 tablespoons sugar (divided use)

2 tablespoons corn syrup

1 teaspoon finely grated orange peel

2 tablespoons orange liqueur (optional)

¾ cup frozen, unsweetened raspberries, slightly thawed

Pre-prep: Chill milk; drain tofu; grate orange peel; thaw raspberries.

1. In a blender or food processor combine milk, tofu, ⅓ cup sugar, corn syrup, orange peel and liqueur, if using; blend until smooth.

2. Place mixture in bowl of ice cream freezer and freeze according to manufacturer's directions.

3. Meanwhile, in a small food processor or blender, process raspberries with remaining 3 tablespoons sugar to a smooth puree. Strain out seeds by working mixture through a sieve with a spoon. When orange mixture is firm, transfer to a container and dribble raspberry puree over it and use a knife to create swirls.

4. Serve immediately or place in freezer until serving time. For the creamiest, smoothest texture, transfer container to the refrigerator 1 hour before serving.

Serves 6

Each serving has approximately:

Cals: 175
Total fat: 1.4 g
Sat fat: 0.3 g

Sodium: 99 mg
Chol: 1.5 mg
Fiber: <1 g

Calcium: 145 mg
Carbs: 30 g
Protein: 8 g

margarita sherbet

More tart than sweet, this is like a creamy frozen margarita. Serve it in sugar- or salt-rimmed martini glasses. For adults only.

Juice of 2 large limes (about ¼ cup)

½ cup sugar

3 tablespoons water

2 tablespoons light corn syrup

2 cups cold 2% reduced-fat milk

½ cup tequila

2 tablespoons triple sec

Sugar

Fresh strawberries and mint for garnish

Pre-prep: Juice limes. At serving time, prepare glasses, strawberries and mint.

1. Mix together lime juice, sugar, water and corn syrup in medium bowl until sugar dissolves. Stir in cold milk.

2. Transfer mixture to ice cream maker and process according to manufacturer's directions. When sherbet is almost set, add tequila and triple sec. Continue to process until frozen. Transfer sherbet to container, cover and place in freezer at least 2 hours. (Can be made 2 days in advance.)

3. To serve, moisten rims of martini glasses, dip in sugar to coat well. Scoop sherbet into glasses. Garnish with fresh strawberry fans and mint leaves.

Serves 4

Each serving has approximately:

Cals: 182
Total fat: 1.6 g
Sat fat: 1 g

Sodium: 50 mg
Chol: 6 mg
Fiber: <1 g

Calcium: 101 mg
Carbs: 28 g
Protein: 3 g

sweetendings

toasted almond brownies

No need to ask if anyone wants seconds on these brownies; they disappear like magic. The almonds toast as the brownies bake.

½ cup European-style or Dutch-processed cocoa

¼ cup water

2 tablespoons canola oil

½ cup light and extra-firm silken tofu or regular block tofu, blended (see Page 17)

1½ cups sugar

1 teaspoon vanilla extract

2 egg whites, lightly beaten

1 egg, lightly beaten

1 cup unbleached flour

¼ teaspoon salt

3 tablespoons chopped or sliced almonds

Pre-prep: Blend tofu; separate 2 eggs (reserve yolks for another use), beat egg whites and one egg together.

1. Preheat oven to 350° F. In a large mixing bowl, whisk together cocoa, water and oil.

2. Add the blended tofu, sugar, vanilla and eggs, mix well; stir in flour and salt.

3. Pour into ungreased 8-inch pan, sprinkle with almonds and bake for 30 minutes. Top will be shiny, but firm; the almonds will be toasted.

Makes 9 (2½-inch) brownies.

Each brownie has approximately:

Cals: 265
Total fat: 6.1 g
Sat fat: 0.8 g

Sodium: 539 mg
Chol: 24 mg
Fiber: 2 g

Calcium: 40 mg
Carbs: 48 g
Protein: 6 g

sweet endings

dark chocolate sorbet

S erious chocoholics will love this dark double-chocolate frozen dessert kissed with orange.

⅔ **cup sugar**

⅔ **cup European-style or Dutch-processed**

1½ **cup water**

¾ **ounce good quality bittersweet chocolate, chopped**

¼ **cup orange juice**

Grated peel of 1 orange

Raspberry Coulis (recipe at left)

Pre-prep: Chop chocolate; grate orange peel. Make Raspberry Coulis.

1. Combine sugar and cocoa in a heavy medium saucepan. Gradually whisk in water, then add chopped chocolate.

2. Cook over low heat until chocolate melts and sugar dissolves. Increase heat to medium-high and boil 1 minute, stirring constantly.

3. Remove from heat; stir in orange juice and peel. Refrigerate until well chilled.

4. Process in ice cream maker according to manufacturer's directions. Serve immediately or transfer to a storage container, cover and freeze overnight to blend flavors. (Can be made 3 days in advance.) Serve on a pool of Raspberry Coulis.

Serves 4 to 6

Each serving has approximately:

Cals: 175	*Sodium: 9 mg*	*Calcium: 24 mg*
Total fat: 2.6 g	*Chol: None*	*Carbs: 37 g*
Sat fat: 1.6 g	*Fiber: 4 g*	*Protein: 3 g*

raspberry coulis

8 ounces unsweetened frozen raspberries

2 tablespoons sugar

1 tablespoon orange liqueur

1. Thaw berries. Place in a food processor or blender with the sugar and process until smooth.

2. Strain through a sieve; press with the back of a spoon to force through. Discard seeds. Stir in liqueur.

sweet endings

strawberry marble cheesecake

This reduced-fat dessert delivers all the flavor and texture cheesecake lovers desire, plus fresh strawberries in every bite.

4 egg whites, room temperature (divided use, see note)

1½ cups graham cracker crumbs (8 whole crackers, crushed)

1½ cups sugar (divided use)

1 tablespoon margarine or butter, melted

Nonstick cooking spray

1 (15-ounce) carton nonfat ricotta cheese

1 (8-ounce) package reduced-fat cream cheese

1 (8-ounce) package nonfat cream cheese

¼ cup cornstarch

2 eggs

¼ teaspoon cream of tartar

1¼ cup finely chopped strawberries, drained

Pre-prep: Bring egg whites to room temperature; crush graham crackers (see tip); melt margarine; chop strawberries.

1. Preheat oven to 350° F. Beat 1 egg white until foamy, add crumbs, ¼ cup sugar and melted margarine; mix well.

2. Coat the bottom of a 9-inch springform pan with cooking spray and press crumbs firmly into bottom of pan. Bake for 10 minutes.

3. Remove from oven and allow to cool. Lower oven setting to 300° F.

4. In a food processor or with an electric mixer, blend ricotta, cream cheeses, cornstarch and 1 cup of sugar. Add the whole eggs; mix well.

5. In a separate bowl, beat remaining egg whites with cream of tartar until foamy; add ¼ cup sugar and beat to soft peaks. Fold egg whites and strawberries into the cheese mixture. Spoon cheese mixture on top of crust.

6. Bake 1 hour; then turn off the oven and leave the cake inside with the door closed 1 more hour. Remove from oven, cool at room temperature for 1 to 2 hours. Refrigerate several hours or overnight.

Serves 12

Each serving has approximately:

Cals: 243	*Sodium: 340 mg*	*Calcium: 253 mg*
Total fat: 5.5 g	*Chol: 48 mg*	*Carbs: 36 g*
Sat fat: 2.8 g	*Fiber: 0.5 g*	*Protein: 12 g*

note

Egg whites whip to a greater volume at room temperature.

tip

Crushing experience: To make graham cracker crumbs, place graham crackers in a large plastic bag or between sheets of wax paper and crush with a rolling pin.

sweet endings

the science behind the recipes

intro

To eat the *Phytopia* way is to savor the rich, lush flavors of a plant-centered cuisine created for sheer pleasure. You need never crack The Science Behind the Recipes to enjoy the many health benefits inherent in this way of eating. But if you're curious about the research that forms the foundation, this section will give you a cook's tour of what is known, what it's based on and what the future holds.

serving sizes:

Many eating guidelines and recommendations, including the Food Guide Pyramid, call for so many servings of certain food groups per day. Here are some commonly recognized single-serving amounts:

One slice of bread, 1 wheat or corn tortilla, 1 ounce of cereal, $^1/_2$ cup cooked pasta, $^1/_2$ bagel or English muffin, 1 cup of raw leafy vegetables such as lettuce or broccoli, $^1/_2$ cup chopped vegetables, 6 ounces vegetable juice such as V-8, 1 wedge of melon, 1 medium apple, 1 medium banana, 1 medium orange, $^1/_2$ cup chopped fruit, 8 ounces milk, 1 cup yogurt, $1^1/_2$ ounces, cheese, 3 ounces lean cooked meat, $^1/_2$ cup cooked beans, 1 egg.

With names like limonene, quercetin and allyl methyl trisulfide, phytochemicals sound more like industrial solvents than key players in a new age of nutrition. (In fact, one phytochemical actually is a grease-cutter found in detergents.) Even the word "phytochemical" sounds vaguely menacing, like something to mop up after a spill.

But nothing could be more natural — or organic. Phytochemicals are simply chemical compounds found in plants: "phyto," the Greek word for plant, coupled with "chemical." With the exception of vitamins C and E and beta carotene, most are not traditional nutrients. Some phytochemicals give fruits their brilliant colors — like lycopene, a pigment that makes tomatoes red and watermelon pink. Some are responsible for aromas — like allium compounds that give us garlic breath. Other phytochemicals discourage animals from chewing on leaves. And some defend against the ravages of oxygen; hence, the term antioxidants, which plants have developed as a survival strategy in an oxygen-rich world.

Numbering in the thousands, phytochemicals promise to change forever the way we think about food, nutrition and health. Scientists who study them say they have the potential to:

- *Slow aging.*
- *Boost immunity.*
- *Prevent, slow or even reverse cancer.*
- *Strengthen our hearts and circulatory systems.*

No one is making specific claims, because there's no certainty that a helping of greens or two carrots a day will keep the doctor away. But like vitamins, phytochemicals may one day add life to our years and years to our lives, especially if they're coupled with lifestyle choices such as exercising regularly and not smoking.

"Phytochemicals are, in a sense, the vitamins and minerals of the 21st century," says Mark Messina, Ph.D., an oft-quoted soyfoods expert and former researcher with the National Cancer Institute's Diet and Cancer Branch. Messina believes phytochemicals will usher in the second Golden Age of Nutrition, an era no less exciting than the period from 1910 to 1960, when most vitamins were identified. During the Golden Age of Nutrition, scientists sought to understand and correct vitamin-deficiency diseases such as rickets and scurvy, all but banishing them from our midst.

research: the promise and the pitfalls

But to understand the science behind the *Phytopia* recipes — what phytochemicals promise and what they do not — you have to grasp the nature of the research, what's been done and what's still left to do.

For the moment, the most persuasive evidence for the benefits of plant-centered cuisine come from several hundred population studies, or epidemiological studies, from places as diverse as rural China, South Louisiana, Colombia and Norway. Although population studies have their limits, the evidence is, in many scientists' estimation, overwhelming:

A plant-centered diet rich in fruits, vegetables and grains enhances your odds for a longer, more healthful life.

This is the most important message of the book. It suggests that we would all be better off shifting animal foods away from the center of the plate and making more room for foods from plants. It doesn't mean giving up meat, though there's nothing wrong with that. It does mean eating more fruits, vegetables and grains and less red meat, as well as fewer foods from animal sources, such as cheese and cream. The point isn't to banish these foods, but to think of them differently.

The idea first captured public interest several years ago when the Mediterranean Diet made headlines, although at the time consumers may not have understood that this was a plant-centered diet. First published in 1980, the Seven Countries Study reported that the inhabitants of a poor Greek island with limited access to medical care nevertheless enjoyed a life expectancy among the highest in the world, with rates of heart disease, some cancers and other diet-related diseases among the lowest.

So much has been written since about the Mediterranean Diet that we sometimes forget it was a snapshot of a specific place and time: Crete in the early 1960s, where eating patterns typified those of much of Greece and southern Italy. It was a diet born of humble circumstance. Seasonal fruits, vegetables and grain products, such as rustic breads, were the foundation. Olive oil was the principle fat; garlic, onions and herbs flavored foods. Fish, poultry and wine were consumed in small to moderate amounts, and red meat was eaten only occasionally. And forget rich desserts; Cretans ate fresh fruit at the end of their meals, if they had dessert at all.

They ate this way because they were poor. Red meat was expensive. Olives were cheap and plentiful. Scientists also believe factors other than diet, such as physical activity and the sense of community that comes with regularly shared meals, may have contributed to the people's robust health. But one contrary finding stood out: The Mediterranean Diet was *not* low in fat. Meanwhile, fat-related diseases — cancer, heart disease, diabetes — were killing people in other parts of the world. This suggested that fat alone might not be the culprit in the so-called diseases of affluence and has led to closer scrutiny of the differences among fats, as well as other factors (1).

All of this came to light through a population study. By documenting broad patterns among living groups of people, population studies provide scientists with big-picture snapshots they can examine for clues

med facts

The Mediterranean diet upon which research is based includes very little saturated fat. Almost absent are meat, poultry, cheese and butter.

about which habits or foods might be linked to specific diseases or their absence. Some scientists compare many such studies, scouring them for trends or for leads to new, more incisive studies. Others begin culling relationships that can be isolated in laboratory or animal studies, reducing broad trends to single, definable, testable events. It's something of a detective game based on educated hunches, because while population studies can show events are correlated, they cannot prove that one is caused by another. The sheer volume of population studies linking fruits and vegetables with reduced risk of disease persuades scientists that there may be a cause-effect relationship.

Another more tightly focused population study that captured headlines in 1995 and 1996 shows how this works. The oft-cited study prompted speculation that lycopene, part of the carotenoid family, might protect against prostate cancer. Until the research was undertaken, data were contradictory on the relationship between vitamin A (which the body manufactures from certain carotenoids), beta carotene (another carotenoid) and the disease.

So Harvard University's Edward Giovannucci (2) sought to examine various carotenoids, vitamin A, fruits, vegetables and the risk of prostate cancer. He conducted the study three times, twice replicating the results before publishing. To the world's amazement, men who ate pizza had less prostate cancer. It made great sound bite, but there was more to it. The data spikes occurred among men who ate an abundance of tomatoes and processed tomato products — such as the sauce on pizza. Tomatoes, tomato sauce, tomato juice and pizza accounted for 82% of the lycopene his subjects ate, which led Giovannucci to suspect that the carotenoid was pivotal.

But the study has been trumpeted across the country as "demonstrating" that lycopene protects against prostate cancer when, in reality, no such relationship has been proven.

The data do suggest he's onto something, however — and it's exciting. "The bottom line is that men [in the study] consuming the high levels of tomatoes had a relative [prostate cancer] risk of .60, which means a 40% reduction," he told a group of tomato growers in 1997 (3). Giovannucci added that lycopene seems to be well absorbed. And, in fact, is the most concentrated carotenoid in the prostate. He continues to refine his research into the lycopene-prostate cancer connection, and other scientists, notably in breast cancer research, are beginning to look more closely at lycopene, too. It may turn out to be the most powerful antioxidant in the carotenoid family.

But no matter how promising a relationship sounds, there's danger in taking studies reported in the media, or even in books like this, at face value. Studies are not meant to be viewed in isolation. To scientists, a single study is an exchange in an ongoing scientific dialogue, not a declaration of some ultimate truth. The same media stories that lauded the "pizza effect" probably didn't have room to point out, for instance, the drawbacks of population studies. In them, researchers depend on people to recall accurately such things as what they eat, how much, if they smoke, how often they exercise — information that can be distorted by everything from a poor memory to a desire to please. When a relationship or correlation does pop up, scientists can only speculate about what forces may be at work and devise new research to test the hunch. Interestingly, in Giovannucci's landmark study, prostate cancer risk also declined among men who reported eating half a cup of strawberries a week. But strawberries contain neither lycopene nor much in the way of other carotenoids (4).

In the big picture, such studies go hand-in-hand with laboratory and animal studies; it's as if the population studies offer broad outlines and lab work fills in the details. Phytochemical lab research has been following two major lines of inquiry. One seeks to discover if there is an optimum balance of foods that provides well being: whether, for instance, eating a serving of spinach a week throughout our lives will protect our eyes from age-related macular degeneration, the leading cause of blindness in people over 65. The other quest is therapeutic: whether phytochemicals may be useful as drugs. For instance, a great deal of research has gone into limonene, and its chemical cousin, perillyl alcohol, and cancer. Among other things, the two monoterpenes show remarkable tumor-shrinking abilities in small rodents. This includes pancreatic tumors, some of the most stubborn and treatment-resistant of all malignancies. Human trials, which are one of the final steps for a promising substance, are now underway with cancer patients, with amounts far exceeding what you would normally consume from foods (5).

The problem with laboratory and animal studies is size and scope. If population studies take big-picture snapshots, lab and animal studies provide microscopic snapshots, sometimes literally. They're so far removed from the real world that it's impossible to know whether a process isolated in a test tube duplicates what happens in humans. And in phytochemical research, for now, these studies make up the bulk of the work. For example, one European study shows that lycopene protects one type of human cell that's important in making antibodies, one of the body's infection fighters. Related research demonstrates that some carotenoids replenish vitamin E's antioxidant capacity (5). This and other studies suggest that lycopene may enhance immunity — but a handful of studies do not an "immune booster" make.

The well-known antioxidant trio, vitamins C and E and beta carotene, has the longest track record in all research arenas. And yet the work has barely begun. Results coming in from many fronts are exciting, baffling and contradictory. For instance, after tracking a group of men and women since 1971, a 1997 Swiss study from the University of Basel found that better memory in old age, as expressed through specific tests, was linked to higher blood levels of beta carotene and vitamin C, but not vitamin E (6). (All but a small percentage of people in the study got

drink to your health?

Guidelines on alcohol consumption conflict, depending on whether you're talking heart disease or cancer. Heart groups cautiously report that one or two glasses of wine a day may enhance heart health, but cancer groups warn that cancer risk can begin to rise with as little as that amount.

their antioxidants from foods, not supplements.) In another long-term population study, the risk of death among middle-aged men in a 24-year follow-up was reduced by a third among those who consumed a diet higher in vitamin C by an amount comparable to that found in one or two oranges a day and higher in beta carotene by one or two carrots a day (7). Meanwhile, the heart-protective properties of vitamin E are well documented (8), and studies continue to refine our understanding of this function as well as expanding into other promising areas, such as the vitamin's effect on immunity (9).

the beta carotene cliff

But look what happened with beta carotene, by now a thoroughly confusing topic if you follow the popular press.

Based on numerous population studies, many scientists felt that beta carotene might protect against lung cancer, just the way lycopene now shows promise against prostate cancer. Beta carotene is a powerful antioxidant that also appears to facilitate cell-to-cell communication, a crucial function often lacking in the cancer. And beta carotene is the body's No. 1 choice for conversion to vitamin A, which, among many functions, may play a role in preventing the development of cancer (10).

With the Alpha-Tocopherol, Beta Carotene Cancer Prevention Study Group, a team of Finnish scientists set out to see if vitamin E and beta carotene would protect 29,000 smokers from cancer. Much to their dismay, the opposite occurred: Lung cancer increased among the men taking beta carotene supplements (11). The Beta Carotene and Retinol Efficiency Trial, a study of 18,000 men and women at high risk for lung cancer, revealed similar problems (12).

With some exceptions, this is where the story ended in the popular press. But discussion among scientists only intensified. One possible explanation for the unexpected results was the beta carotene itself: Taking a synthetic carotenoid in a pill isn't the same as eating a carotenoid-rich diet. It's been suggested that six years of supplements may not undo a lifetime of smoking, or that 20 to 30 milligrams a day is too low a dose — although population studies have indicated protection at lower levels for nonsmokers (13).

But one of the most significant studies on beta carotene to date, indeed a turning point, was barely a blip on the media screen when it was published in 1996. 22,000 U.S. male physicians participated in a 12-year study wherein the test group took 50 milligrams of beta carotene every other day and the control group received a placebo. Most were nonsmokers, an important and major difference from the previous studies. The results: No effect. None. Looking at cancer, heart disease and deaths from all causes, the scientists observed no effect, positive or negative, with beta carotene supplementation (14). But it was under-reported

because such a "null" finding isn't as exciting as news of contrary
results.

Not that this study explains what happened in Finland. But it does
suggest that beta carotene's "negative" effect may be unique to smokers.
More recent research has suggested that perhaps another nutrient holds
part of the answer. Smoking depletes vitamins C and E, and in the
absence of vitamin C, a potentially harmful form of beta carotene can
accumulate (15).

But clearly, beta carotene's star has begun to fade and lycopene is
increasingly gaining research attention. Yet debate and research about
beta carotene continues, for while it may not be the powerhouse that
once was postulated, it still shows many promising characteristics. For
now, some scientists suggest that smokers avoid beta carotene supplements until more is learned. But this shouldn't stop anyone, smokers
included, from eating lots of carotenoid-rich fruits and vegetables.

For that matter, some phytochemicals have negative properties —
remember, many evolved to defend plants against the elements and preda-
tors. Some phytochemicals act as pro-oxidants under certain conditions,
meaning they promote oxidative damage. Some are rich in nitrates, which
can be building blocks for carcinogens, although the antioxidants present
in the same foods are thought the counteract the formation of these (10).
Some phytochemicals are toxic in large amounts.

Furthermore, scientists don't know how much is absorbed by our
bodies from foods, not even with well-studied substances like vitamin E.
Nor do they know how much foods contain (16). This depends on the
plant species, soil and climate conditions, transit time to market and other
factors.

We've taken this modest tour through the labyrinth of science to
offer context for the information that follows. When you read
"Glutathione, found in onions, may detoxify cancer-causing substances,"
there may be two or 200 studies suggesting this function, each in a
minute way. But the picture is so far from complete that it would be
unwise to take any action beyond adopting a more plant-centered diet
and, perhaps, adding a vitamin E supplement.

the phyto map

Even though there are thousands of phytochemicals, a far smaller
number are biologically active in humans. Identifying the most promising
of these has been a major focus of the past 15 years. In that time, cancer
research has been the most prolific, followed by cardiovascular work.
Some of the findings about immunity come from cancer research, as
some phytochemicals have been found, at least in the laboratory, to prevent cancer. And while antioxidants are pivotal in all areas of research,
they are fundamental to the concept that phytochemicals slow aging.

aging and immunity: the antioxidant connection

From a diet standpoint, antioxidant theory suggests that eating more foods rich in antioxidants will bolster immune forces and slow aging. At the 1996 United Nations and World Health Organization First Joint Conference on Healthy Aging, one scientist said the life span of the average person might be effectively extended by increasing antioxidant intake (17).

But exactly what transpires in your body after you swallow antioxidants in a mouthful of carrots is still a mystery. Basic research tells us some antioxidants are used up in chemical reactions, while others are renewed or work synergistically to maintain their antioxidant capacity. Vitamin C, for instance, appears to extend the antioxidizing life of vitamin E, beta carotene and lycopene to prevent LDL oxidation, a significant factor in cardiovascular health (18).

Although we need oxygen to live, we pay a price for it. Oxidation occurs all around us when the element in various forms reacts with other substances. When you slice an apple and it turns brown, the surface is oxidizing. Squeeze lemon juice onto the apple and antioxidants in the lemon juice tie up the oxygen and retard enzyme activity, preventing the characteristic brown discoloration. Rust, fire and rancidity are other forms of oxidation.

In our bodies, free radicals are the damaging, oxidizing molecules. These are given off routinely by cells as energy is produced — like exhaust from an internal combustion engine. Free radicals also come from outside the body — from real auto and industrial emissions, cigarette smoke, sunlight and other sources. So our cells are bombarded with free radicals from without and from within all the time. These highly reactive forms of oxygen — which include singlet oxygen, nitric oxide and peroxyl radicals among others — carry an unpaired electron and are drawn like magnets to the nearest molecule that can relieve this imbalance. The result is often cellular damage, minute but cumulative.

Polyunsaturated fatty acids, which are part of every cell membrane, are especially vulnerable to free radical damage; so are cell proteins and the genetic material (DNA) in the cell's nucleus. DNA damage is a precursor to cancer.

Antioxidants, our cells' first line of defense against free radicals, work to mop up the offending molecules — to react with them and render them harmless — but aren't 100% effective. And the system feeds upon itself: The more free radical damage, the less efficient the energy-producing machinery; the less efficient the machinery, the more free radicals released. Again, think of an automobile: The older and crankier the engine and the less care it has received, the more emissions it produces and the less efficiently it runs.

Vitamin C, which one scientist calls "the first line of defense in human plasma," is the most powerful water-soluble antioxidant (19).

---

the riddle of immunity

When a group of elderly people who had lost some of their sense of taste and smell ate flavor/aroma-enhanced foods, their immunity improved – and it wasn't just because they were eating more. Schiffman and Warwick, whose 1993 study was published in *Physiology and Behavior*, speculated that the enhanced foods may have affected endorphins in a positive way.

Vitamin E is the most powerful fat-soluble antioxidant. Dozens of other phytochemicals also possess antioxidant properties.

As we age, our immune system — a complex of specialized cells, antibodies and proteins — responds less vigorously to invaders. Many scientists believe oxidative damage is at the heart of premature aging as well as the diseases that develop later in life, such as cancer, heart disease, cataracts and brain dysfunction.

Still, the aging-immunity-antioxidant connection is largely, though not entirely, theoretical. Limited research on immunity done with older people and vitamin E, for instance, has been supportive. In a 1997 study, vitamin E improved immunity in a group of healthy older adults. Those who took 200 IUs daily for the four-month period showed the greatest gains. Researchers compared this to subjects who took 60 IUs, which is double the RDA, and those who took 800 IUs, a "mega" dose. In all groups, immunity improved, but it was greatest in the middle group (9). In another study, some of the most debilitating symptoms of Alzheimer's Disease were delayed among patients taking 2,000 milligrams of vitamin E a day (20).

The carotenoids, also potent free radical fighters, are believed to play an important role in preventing cancer (see "Cancer"), another disease associated with growing older. They include primarily alpha carotene, beta carotene, lycopene, cryptoxanthin, lutein and zeaxanthin. Some scientists now believe lycopene is the most powerful carotenoid antioxidant, and research is underway with both prostate and breast cancer because of its potential (3). In animal studies, carotenoids have also been shown to protect the skin from redness and damage after exposure to ultraviolet radiation (which mimics sunlight) (21); this, too, suggests though does not prove a protective function. Giovannucci speculates that tomatoes developed the red pigment lycopene as a defense against the ravages of sunlight (3).

Lutein and zeaxanthin appear to play an important role in preventing age-related macular degeneration, the leading cause of blindness in people over 65. The irreversible disease that affects several million Americans occurs when the 3-millimeter-wide macula (part of the retina) loses its ability to discern images in sharp detail. It's called "age-related" because, again, it is associated with growing older. Lutein and zeaxanthin, two yellow carotenoids, are believed to filter out harmful blue light and to scavenge free radicals that form in response to sunlight (22). In population studies, people who eat greater amounts of spinach and collard greens, rich sources of lutein and zeaxanthin, are far less susceptible to the disease (23).

Other indirect evidence of anti-aging comes from additional eye research. Vitamins C and E and carotenoids reduce the risk of cataracts, possibly because they work as antioxidants in the lens of the eye. Research also shows that damage to the lens increases as antioxidants are depleted (24). One study compared people with cataracts to those without; the latter group took significantly more vitamin supplements, especially C and E (25).

HIV and AIDS research echo these themes, suggesting patients' immunity is compromised when antioxidants are deficient. A limited number of lab, animal and preliminary human studies with vitamin E and beta carotene also suggest that these antioxidants in particular may slow the progression of HIV to AIDS, as well as decrease some of the symptoms associated with the disease (26).

Other promising and potent antioxidants attracting scientists' attention include the phenolic compounds, a huge group that includes flavonoids (substances studied in onions, red wine and green tea), and thiols, which include gluathione. In addition, nutrients such as zinc, folic acid and selenium may play roles in strengthening immunity.

eat less, live longer?

But perhaps the most tantalizing support for the antioxidant theory of aging comes from calorie-restriction studies. Instead of looking at ways to increase antioxidant intake, calorie-restriction scientists grapple with ways to slow down free–radical production in the first place. By restricting calories in experimental animals, they slow the cellular energy-producing processes that release damaging compounds. In creatures as diverse as water fleas, spiders, guppies, rats and monkeys, studies have demonstrated consistently that such a diet lengthens life and delays the onset of late-life diseases, affecting both quality and quantity of life. For example, among white rats, both average and maximum life spans were increased by 50%. Photographs of the animals show dramatic differences. Scientists hesitate to say what this means for humans — indeed some of us might chafe at the thought of a longer life with less gustatory pleasure — but two studies are underway with longer-lived primates (27), which will bring clinical trials to the human doorstep.

cancer: you have the power

Contrary to widely held beliefs, cancer isn't something that just "happens" to you.

For the first time, we're beginning to see that lifestyle choices have a tremendous impact on susceptibility. About a third of all cancer deaths are now known to be diet-related — no small number when you consider that smoking also accounts for a third of cancer deaths (28). Further, it's been estimated that up to 70 percent of all cancers may be diet-related (10). Genetics and lack of exercise also play a role, as is the case with heart disease, but the implications for individual empowerment are enormous.

Our bodies are bombarded daily with carcinogens, which are con-

stantly being swept up by internal defenses, from detoxifying enzymes
to antioxidants. Phytochemicals, both as antioxidants and by other
means, interrupt the chain of events leading to cancer in many ways.
Some appear to assist the enzymes that disarm and block carcinogens in
the first place, so the bad guys never get a grip on the body. Some help
repair damaged DNA before the cell can multiply or mutate, returning
the cell to its normal healthy state. Others prevent damaged cells from
proliferating and becoming cancerous or, once cancerous, from migrat-
ing to other parts of the body (5).

A great deal of research has been devoted to fruits, vegetables and
cancer prevention, which provides indirect, but persuasive evidence for
phytochemicals' benefits. In 1996, Kristi Steinmetz, Ph.D., R.D., and
John Potter, M.D., Ph.D., assembled more than 200 population studies
and nearly two dozen animal studies for a state-of-the-research overview
(10). It updated and reinforced an earlier survey, in which they speculated that cancer "may be a disease of maladaptation" resulting from too
few plant foods in our diets.

Summing up in the newer study, they wrote: "The evidence for a
protective effect of greater vegetable and fruit consumption is consistent
for cancers of the stomach, esophagus, lung, oral cavity and pharynx,
endometrium, pancreas and colon. The types of vegetables or fruit that
most often appear to be protective against cancer are raw vegetables, followed by allium vegetables [the onion-garlic family], carrots, green vegetables, cruciferous vegetables [the broccoli-kale family] and tomatoes."

Worldwide, stomach cancer has gotten the most attention, and
research shows that eating citrus fruits and vegetables, especially raw
and green vegetables, clearly reduces the risk of developing the disease.
Data for protection against lung cancer also are overwhelming — for
fruits and vegetables in general and green vegetables and tomatoes in
particular. For mouth and esophageal cancers, green vegetables and citrus fruits score high; tomatoes stand out against esophageal cancer.

For other cancer sites, data are less abundant or less consistent.
Even so, the studies show trends, Steinmetz and Potter say: Carrots
appear to offer some protection against oral cancers; vegetables, especially raw and green vegetables, against colon cancer; cruciferous vegetables against rectal cancer; fruit, green vegetables and carrots against
breast cancer; and green vegetables and carrots against bladder cancer.

Although Steinmetz and Potter cite hundreds of studies, there are
hundreds more, large and small, devoted to understanding what it is in
plants that may prevent, slow and even reverse malignancies. Most are
just beginning to unravel the basic biochemistry, and more than two
dozen phytochemicals are the subject of intense scrutiny. Here are some
of the most promising:

■ Found in the cruciferous (broccoli-kale) family, dithiolthiones
and isothiocyanates are prime anticancer candidates. The American
Health Foundation's Dr. Stephen S. Hecht says isothiocyanates are

sprout power

Broccoli sprouts are loaded with a concentrated form of sulforophane, one of the important anticancer organosulfides. This was reported in the journal *Proceedings of the National Academy of Sciences* in 1997 by a Johns Hopkins University team headed by Dr. Paul Talaly.

"among the most effective chemopreventive agents known," meaning they prevent or reverse the changes that transform cells with damaged DNA into cancerous ones. Isothiocyanates also increase the activity of enzymes that detoxify carcinogens, so less of a carcinogen is available to cause harm. Isothiocyanates have been shown to prevent lung, mammary, esophageal, liver, small intestine, colon and bladder cancers in rats (5). Sulforophane looks especially potent.

■ These are part of a larger group of phytochemicals called organosulfides; other promising organosulfides are found in the allium family, where garlic and onions are singled out for special properties. One scientist says eating allium vegetables may considerably reduce the risk of stomach cancer. In garlic, diallyl sulfide and allyl methyl trisulfide appear to aid the enzymes that detoxify carcinogens. They also have antibacterial properties (29). In the stomach, they may prevent or slow the conversion of nitrates, a key substance in a chain of events that can produce carcinogens. (Vegetables contain a lot of nitrates, but vitamins C and E and phenolic compounds probably render them harmless, write Steinmetz and Potter.) (10) Garlic grown in selenium-enriched soil gets a double dose of cancer-fighting power: from garlic and from the trace mineral, which is also being studied in relation to cancer (5).

■ Onions contain additional cancer-fighting compounds. They're the richest source of quercetin, the most common and most studied flavonoid. It's a powerhouse: Besides possessing important heart-protective properties, the antioxidant is believed to affect cancer in several ways, from "trapping" carcinogens to influencing stages of development. Onions also contain glutathione, an important thiol antioxidant, and the flavonoid kaempferol; both may help with detoxification (29).

■ Flavonoids, a subset of phenolic compounds, are ubiquitous in plants. Quercetin and others in green tea and wine are of particular interest in relation to cancer. In mice and rats, for instance, extracts of green tea have been shown to protect against cancers of the esophagus, digestive tract, liver and other organs (30). But population studies involving green tea have been equivocal (5), so the implications for humans still aren't known. (Some black tea also contains phenolic compounds, though in some cases they are oxidized out in manufacturing.)

■ Armed with an arsenal of anticancer functions, carotenoids are a family of powerful antioxidants found in dark yellow and orange fruits and vegetables and deep green vegetables. Beta carotene and alpha carotene (carrots are the No. 1 source) appear to protect against the progression of cancer, whereas others carotenoids may be more effective at earlier stages (31, 10). Carotenoids may work against cancer by boosting the immune system and supporting the enzymes that detoxify carcinogens. Beta carotene and lycopene both have been shown to affect intercellular communication, which may prevent damaged cells from becoming malignant. And both animal and population studies suggest various carotenoids may protect against specific cancers: lycopene against prostate cancer; lutein, zeaxanthin, alpha carotene and beta carotene against lung cancer; beta carotene against oral cancers; and cryptoxanthin against cervical cancer (22).

■ Another group of flavonoids, isoflavones, which are transformed into estrogenlike compounds in the intestines, are found almost exclusively in soybeans (and therefore soyfoods) and play a special role in hormone-related cancers. Called phytoestrogens ("plant" estrogens), they are 250 to 1,000 times weaker than the body's own estrogen. Some are chemically similar to tamoxifen, a drug used to treat breast cancer. Genistein, the subject of more than 1,000 studies, ties up the estrogen receptors on cells so that the body's own estrogen can't attach to them. Genistein also may slow cancer by interfering with growth signals. Genistein and biochanin A, another isoflavone, also may help reset a cell's "death" program, which goes awry in cancer (10). (Normal cells are programmed to die naturally at a certain point.) The research of Dr. Stephen Barnes at the University of Alabama at Birmingham suggests that two (8-ounce) servings of soy milk a day may offer some protection against breast cancer (5).

■ One of the indoles found in cruciferous vegetables, indole-3-carbinol, may also protect against hormone-related cancers (10), as do lignans, which also are converted to compounds with estrogenlike qualities. Lignans are found primarily in whole-grain foods, vegetables, fruits and some berries.

■ Two monoterpenes — limonene, and its metabolite, perillyl alcohol — are already being tested in humans, as mentioned earlier, because of their performance against malignancies in animals. Most abundant in orange peel oil, limonene gives oranges and lemons their citrusy aroma; it's used widely to scent products such as furniture polish and dish soap; it's also a great grease-cutter (32).

Other plant compounds under investigation for anticancer activity include: coumarins, phytosterols, saponins, vitamins C and E, protease inhibitors, dietary fiber, phytic acid and folic acid (10).

cardiovascular disease: health in a heartbeat

Although heart disease remains the leading cause of death in America, the death rate from heart disease— the number of lives claimed per thousand — has dropped by about a third since 1980 (33). Part of the reason is improved treatment, but in that time public awareness has changed, too. We now understand the fat-heart connection, hammered home by the American Heart Association and others: No more than 30% of calories in our diet should come from fat and no more than 10% from saturated fat. We know there's a diet-cholesterol connection, too.

At least we assume these things are true. But just when Americans seem to be absorbing this public health message, along comes the French Paradox to complicate the picture.

the soy connection

Genistein, an isoflavone from soybeans, is of particular interest in women's health because some of it is converted in the intestines to a compound that acts as a weak estrogen (phytoestrogen). Although required for normal functioning, too much estrogen can increase the risk of hormone-related cancers, especially breast cancer. Phytoestrogens can lock into estrogen receptors on a cell, effectively blocking out some of the real estrogen. Population studies of women in Japan, who eat a lot of soyfoods, suggest that it may prevent breast cancer as well as reduce or prevent the symptoms of menopause, such as hot flashes, but this has not been tested in a double-blind controlled study. Soyfoods include soybeans, tofu, soy milk, miso and tempeh. Genistein may also affect prostate cancer and may minimize loss of bone density (this, too, has yet to be directly tested)(34).

High cholesterol, high blood pressure, smoking and excess weight are all risk factors for heart disease. Yet the French — who eat nearly four times as much butter (swimming in cholesterol-raising saturated fat) and three times as much lard (same story) as Americans, whose cholesterol and blood pressure are higher than ours, who are just as overweight and smoke about as much as Americans do — die far less frequently from heart disease (35).

Like the Mediterranean Diet before it, the so-called French Paradox prompted a double-take. And when scientists postulated that red wine might be part of the reason, *60 Minutes* — and a nation — embraced the beverage. Although several factors in the French diet may ultimately prove to be heart-protective, the flavonoids (phenolic compounds) in red wine, fruits and vegetables are prime suspects (36).

Scientists are trying to figure out how these phenolic compounds and other phytochemicals affect two fundamental processes concerned with heart health: the prevention of LDL oxidation — which directly and indirectly involves antioxidants — and the ability of a compound to slow blood clotting (platelet aggregation), making blood less "sticky."

In truth, the so-called "bad" LDL cholesterol is bad only when the body makes too much or can't remove it efficiently. The excess becomes an easy target for free radicals, and it is oxidized LDL that contributes to plaque buildup inside artery walls. This eventually constricts vessels, decreasing flexibility and blood flow. Blood that is less sticky or is slow to clot will have a better chance of moving through even narrowed arteries, but only to a point. When plaque buildup chokes off the arteries that feed the heart, a heart attack results. In the brain, it's one kind of stroke.

The most important phytochemical in this process is a familiar one.

"Of all [the] nutrients with cardio-protective potential, the case is most convincing for vitamin E," say the authors of the University of California at Berkeley *Wellness Letter*, whose editorial board is made up of health and nutrition experts. Vitamin E has been the subject of hundreds of studies, both by itself and in tandem with other antioxidants, and a number of these studies support a heart-protective function. The amount required varies. Two large population studies, the Nurses Health Study and the Health Professionals Follow-up Study, suggest from 100 to 200 IUs may be protective (37). But human trials also have indicated that as much as 400 IUs may be needed to induce the antioxidant effect (38).

Vitamin E protects primarily by preventing LDL oxidation, with this advantage over most other antioxidants: It is carried through the bloodstream by the LDL molecule itself, where it is in a unique position to protect the LDL's vulnerable polyunsaturated fatty acid. In lab studies, LDL oxidation works on a priority sequence: First, the vitamin E is consumed (oxidized), followed by beta carotene and lycopene. Only when these are exhausted is the LDL oxidized. When vitamin C is added to the mix, the antioxidant capacity of vitamin E and beta carotene is extended

almost tenfold (18). In addition, vitamin E may reduce blood clotting.

Outside of some population studies, virtually all vitamin E research has used supplements. But to get the same amount from foods, you'd have to eat too much fat. So even the most conservative health groups are beginning to suggest that vitamin E might be the exception to the general recommendation that nutrients be acquired from the foods we eat, not the pills we pop. (Most experts do say that, with this exception, phytochemicals should come from foods, not supplements. There are indications of synergistic effects that simply aren't understood yet.)

Of the eight types of vitamin E, alpha tocopherol is the most common. Unlike most vitamins, the natural form may be superior to synthetic. Further, research reported in 1997 suggests that gamma tocopherol, the most abundant form of E in foods, may complement the action of alpha tocopherol (39). You can get gamma in mixed tocopherol supplements, but not as a single-substance supplement. The best food sources are those made with soy oil, which include many salad dressings, margarine and baked goods; sunflower seeds and oil also contain a fair amount.

As for the other two of the "big three" antioxidants — vitamin C and beta carotene — the cardiovascular research has not been as consistent or dramatic, though in general vitamin C appears to protect against plaque buildup in arteries, possibly because of its E-enhancing function (18). The Western Electric Study of 1,550 normal men showed that eating foods rich in vitamin C and beta carotene over several decades reduced the risk of death from all causes (7). But if you'll recall, in the 12-year study of 22,000 U.S. male physicians mentioned earlier, scientists observed no effect on risk of death, positive or negative, for beta carotene and cancer or heart disease (14).

Beyond the big three, phenolic compounds are among the phytochemicals getting the closest look in relation to heart disease. This huge family of potent antioxidants includes lignans (found especially in flax seed and other grain products), flavonoids (abundant in red wine, green tea and onions), phenolic acids (which include ellagic acid, tannic acid and vanillin) and hydroxycinnamic acid derivatives (caffeic, chlorogenic and ferulic acids, curcumin and coumarins). Ellagic acid is abundant in berries, but its bioavailability is questionable. Tannic acid gives wine and tea their pucker power. Coumarins are abundant in citrus fruits. In addition, red wine and peanuts contain resveratrol, a phenolic fungicide that some scientists believe may contribute heart-protective properties.

Flavonoids were singled out in a 1997 American Heart Association statement on heart disease and phytochemicals published in the journal *Circulation*. In general, flavonoids have gotten high marks for heart protection in population studies, the authors say (40).

For instance, the Zutphen Elderly Study showed that the risk of heart disease decreased as flavonoid consumption increased for a group of 800 men between ages 65 and 84 living in Zutphen, a small industrial town in the Netherlands. The research was based on data collected for

E is for exercise

In a small number of experiments with elite athletes, one scientist has observed that vitamins C and E appear to help muscles recover more quickly from the oxidative stress that comes with vigorous exercise. But it does not improve performance. One study used cyclists; another, long-distance runners (41,42).

the Seven Countries Study, and, for the Zutphen men, the main flavonoid sources were tea, onions, apples and wine (36, 43).

Some flavonoids are voracious free radical scavengers and thus strong inhibitors of LDL oxidation. Some also slow blood clotting and reduce blood's stickiness. Quercetin, especially abundant in onions but also found in wine and other fruits and vegetables, is a potent inhibitor of LDL oxidation. In addition, some of the flavonoids in soybeans — isoflavones — lower cholesterol. And their conversion to estrogen-mimicking compounds, so vital in cancer protection, also protect the heart (40, 43).

Phytosterols, also mentioned in the AHA statement, lower cholesterol. Found in almonds, cashews, peanuts, sesame seeds, sunflower seeds, whole wheat, corn, soybeans and many vegetable oils, plant sterols may be the reason monounsaturated and polyunsaturated oils have cholesterol-lowering properties, the authors say. Drawing on studies that date to the 1950s, they single out three important ones: beta-sitosterol, stagmasterol and campesterol (40).

The other broad category of phytochemicals mentioned by the AHA statement is the organosulfur compounds found in the allium family (onions-garlic). Much of the research has been based on garlic and garlic oil, which have been shown to lower cholesterol and blood pressure as well as slow blood clotting. The authors say that diallyl sulfide is the most active compound in garlic (40).

Unlike cancer research, in which population studies have looked directly at fruits, vegetables and disease, only a few cardiovascular studies outside the Seven Countries Study have taken the same direct approach with these foods. Here are two of interest:

■ In one, eating fruits and vegetables appeared to protect against stroke. For each additional three servings of fruits and vegetables a day, risk of stroke dropped by almost 25% among healthy middle-aged men who were also part of the larger Framingham (heart) Study. Scientists speculated that antioxidants reduced LDL cholesterol and that folate, another beneficial plant nutrient, might have played a role (44).

■ Finally, in the DASH study (Dietary Approaches to Stop Hypertension), a diet rich in fruits and vegetables lowered blood pressure. But with this caveat: It did no good to merely substitute fruits and vegetables for snacks and sweets in a typical American diet. Although that might be a step in the right direction, total fat reduction was required — in this case from 37% of calories to 27% — to make a difference. This was achieved in the study primarily by also using low-fat dairy products and curtailing red meat and added fats, such as salad dressing (45).

So phytochemicals are no panacea, no cure for what ails the world. And yet the potential for improving health, based on research to this point, is enormous. If this is the first you've heard or read about phytochemicals, it will not be the last. In the next century, they promise to become as familiar as vitamins and minerals. And, perhaps, just as important to the quality of our lives.

foods and their phytochemicals

Here's a list of fruits, vegetables, nuts and grains and some of the phytochemicals and other pertinent nutrients they contain. But the exact amount, how much our bodies absorb and how much is optimum for good health in most cases isn't known. The actual phytochemical content depends on many factors, including plant variety, soil composition, how the crop was grown, how it was stored and processed — even, in the case of broccoli, what part of the plant you eat. The carotenoid content of foods is better understood than for other phytochemicals, thanks to the establishment in 1993 of the U.S. Department of Agriculture-National Cancer Institute Carotenoid Food Composition Data Base.

Absence from this list doesn't mean a food contains no phyto-chemicals; it may simply mean the food hasn't been assessed or investigated in studies. Some phytochemicals, those in the flavonoid family for example, are found in virtually all fruits and vegetables. Most vegetables and herbs also contain saponins. For optimum benefit, until more is known, the strongest scientific evidence supports a varied diet rich in foods from plant sources.

Acorn squash: Carotenoids.

Alfalfa sprouts: In one study, their antioxidant activity against three specific free radicals was shown to be relatively high (46).

Almonds: One of the richest sources of alpha-tocopherol vitamin E. Phytosterols; high in monounsaturated fats; dietary fiber (with skin).

Apples: Quercetin and kaempferol (flavonols); dietary fiber (including peel).

Apricots: Beta carotene. Dried are an especially rich source.

Artichokes: Silymarin (flavonoid), modest carotenoids, vitamin C.

Asparagus: Modest source of the carotenoids lutein, zeaxanthin and beta carotene; glutathione; folic acid. Modest source of alpha-tocopherol vitamin E.

Avocados: High in monounsaturated fat, modest source of alpha-tocopherol vitamin E.

Bananas: Fiber. One South American study of vegetables, fruits and colon cancer risk showed bananas to be the most protective (47).

Beans (legumes): Flavonoids, dietary fiber, saponins, protease inhibitors.

Beets: In one study, their antioxidant activity against three specific free radicals was shown to be moderately high (46).

Beet greens: The carotenoids beta carotene, lutein and xeazanthin.

Bell peppers: Good source of plant phenols, especially coumarins, and terpenes. Also contain glucarates, vitamin C. Reds are a moderately good source of flavonoids and some carotenoids, especially lutein and zeaxanthin. In one study, reds also showed moderately high antioxidant activity against one kind of free radical (46).

Berries: Quercetin and kaempferol (flavonols), some carotenoids.

Blackberries: Fair amount of ellagic acid (bioavailability is questionable).

Blueberries: Caffeic and ferulic acid (phenolic acids).

Bok choy: A cruciferous vegetable rich in dithiolthiones, isothiocyanates, flavonoids and organosulfides. It also contains glucarates, terpenes and phenolic compounds such as coumarins.

Brazil nuts: Vitamin E, selenium.

Broccoli: A cruciferous vegetable. Organosulfides, flavonoids, indoles, dithiolthiones, isothiocyanates, carotenoids (highest concentration in the leaves, more in the florets than the stems), quercetin and keampferol (flavonols), glucarates, terpenes, phenolic compounds such as coumarins, protease inhibitors, vitamin C, dietary fiber and selenium. Modest source of alpha tocopherol vitamin E. Cooking may increase the accessibility of the carotenoids and indoles. In one study, broccoli's antioxidant activity against one specific free radical was high (46). Calcium from broccoli is better absorbed than from milk (48).

Brussels sprouts: A cruciferous vegetable rich in organosulfides, dithiolthiones, isothiocyanates, flavonoids, protease inhibitors and vitamin C. Modest source of the carotenoids lutein and zeaxanthin. They also contain glucarates, coumarins and other phenolic acids, and terpenes. In one study, their antioxidant activity against two specific free radicals was high (46).

Cabbage: A cruciferous vegetable. Indoles, dithiolthiones, isothiocyanates, flavonoids, organosulfides, glucarates, coumarins and other phenolic acids, terpenes, selenium and vitamin C. Chinese (Napa) cabbage is relatively high in absorbable calcium.

Canola oil: Monounsaturated fats, vitamin E. A non-fish source of essential fatty acids, from which omega-3s are derived.

Cantaloupe: Beta carotene, vitamin C.

Caraway: Monoterpenes in seeds and oil.

Carrots: Carotenoids (major dietary contributor of both alpha carotene and beta carotene), plant phenols (especially flavonoids), terpenes.

Cashew nuts: Phytosterols.

Cauliflower: A cruciferous vegetable rich in indoles, dithiolthiones, isothiocyanates, flavonoids and organosulfides. It also contains glucarates, coumarins and other phenolic compounds, terpenes and vitamin C.

Celery: Phenolic compounds (especially flavonoids and coumarins), terpenes. Also the carotenoids lutein and zeaxanthin.

Cereal grains: Many phenolic compounds (especially flavonoids and coumarins), glucarates, carotenoids and terpenes. Corn, wheat, oats, rice and barley are moderately good sources of phytic acid. Wheat germ oil is one of the richest sources of vitamin E.

Cherries: Quercetin and kaempferol (flavonols), perillyl alcohol.

Chile peppers: Modest source of carotenoids, especially lutein and zeaxanthin, some beta carotene, vitamin C.

Chives: Organosulfides, modest source of the carotenoids lutein and zeaxanthin. Richer source: dried or dehydrated.

Citrus fruits: Contain flavonoids (sometimes referred to as bioflavonoids, an older research term), limonene and perillyl alcohol, glucarates, carotenoids, coumarins and teriterpenes, vitamin C.

Cloves: Contain vanillin, a phenolic acid.

Collard greens: A cruciferous vegetable. The carotenoids lutein, zeaxanthin and beta carotene. In one study, eating a lot of collard greens or spinach was associated with reduced risk of the leading cause of blindness over 65 (23). Also, dithiolthiones, isothiocyanates, flavonoids, organosulfides, glucarates, coumarins and other phenolic compounds and terpenes.

Corn: Phytosterols, protease inhibitors, modest source of the carotenoids lutein and zeaxanthin.

Cottonseed oil: Vitamin E, about equally divided between alpha- and gamma-tocopherol.

grill talk

Marinating chicken before grilling decreases the amount of some carcinogens found on cooked birds. This comes from a report presented at the 1997 meeting of the American Chemical Society by Dr. Mark Knize, et al., from the Lawrence Livermore National Laboratory at Livermore, Calif.

Cranberries: Ellagic acid (though it's not readily absorbed), rich source of other flavonoids.

Cruciferous vegetables: These include bok choy, broccoli, brussels sprouts, cabbage, cauliflower, collard greens, kale, kohlrabi, mustard greens, rutabaga, turnips, watercress. All are rich in isothiocyanates, flavonoids and organosulfides. They also contain glucarates, coumarins and other phenolic compounds, and terpenes. In one study, many members of the family showed high antioxidant activity against three specific free radicals (46).

Cucumbers: Protease inhibitors, phenolic compounds.

Dill: Monoterpenes, moderate carotenoids.

Eggplant: Good source of phenolic compounds (especially flavonoids and coumarins) and monoterpenes. Also glucarates and teriterpenes.

Endive: Flavonoids, also the carotenoids lutein and zeaxanthin, plus beta carotene.

Escarole: The carotenoids lutein and zeaxanthin, plus beta carotene.

Fennel bulb: Moderate beta carotene.

Fenugreek: Coumarins.

Flax seed and flour: Extremely rich source of lignans. Also flavonoids, coumarins and other phenolic compounds. The oil is a non-fish source of essential fatty acids, from which omega-3s are derived.

Garlic: Organosulfides (notably diallyl sulfide and allyl methyl trisulfide), which may be destroyed by cooking. Also phenolic acids, monoterpenes. Garlic shows strong antibacterial activity. In one study, it had the highest antioxidant activity by weight against one kind of free radical (46).

Grapefruit: Along with other citrus fruits, rich in flavonoids, as well as the monoterpene limonene. Also vitamin C, glucarates, carotenoids, coumarins and other phenolic compounds. Pink grapefruit is moderately high in lycopene.

Grapes: Flavonoids, also caffeic, ferulic and ellagic acids (phenolic acids), and resveratrol, a phenolic fungicide. Ellagic acid may not be absorbed.

Guava: Lycopene.

Hazelnuts: Rich in monounsaturated fat; some vitamin E.

Kale: A cruciferous vegetable extremely rich in the carotenoids lutein and zeaxanthin, with less beta carotene. A good source of quercetin and kaempferol (flavonols). Rich in dithiolthiones, isothiocyanates, other flavonoids and organosulfides. It also contains glucarates, coumarins and other phenolic compounds, terpenes and vitamin C. In one study of 22 vegetables and green and black tea, the antioxidant activity of kale against two specific free radicals was among the highest (46). Calcium from kale better absorbed than from milk (48).

Kiwi: Vitamin C.

Kohlrabi: A cruciferous vegetable. Rich in dithiolthiones, isothiocyanates, flavonoids and organosulfides. It also contains glucarates, coumarins and other phenolic compounds, and terpenes.

Leeks: Organosulfides, some carotenoids.

Legumes: A lesser source of isoflavones, rich in dietary fiber.

Lemons: Along with other citrus fruits, rich in flavonoids, as well as the monoterpenes limonene and perillyl alcohol. Also vitamin C, glucarates, coumarins and other phenolic compounds, and teriterpenes.

Lentils: Selenium, fiber, protease inhibitors, folic acid.

Lettuce: A moderately good source of flavonoids.

Licorice root: Phenolic compounds, especially flavonoids.

Lima beans: Rich in phytic acid.

Limes: Along with other citrus fruits, rich in flavonoids, as well as the monoterpenes limonene and perillyl alcohol. Also vitamin C, glucarates, coumarins and other phenolic compounds, and teriterpenes.

Macadamia nuts: In one small study, macadamia nuts neither raised nor lowered total cholesterol, but did improve the LDL:HDL ratio (49).

Mango: Beta carotene and cryptoxanthin (carotenoids), vitamins C and E.

Mustard: Curcumin (phenolic compound).

Mustard greens: A cruciferous vegetable rich in dithiolthiones, isothiocyanates, the carotenoids lutein and zeaxanthin, some beta carotene,

long-lived oils

Always store oils in the refrigerator and seeds and nuts in the freezer because the oils are easily oxidized, initiating rancidity.

flavonoids and organosulfides. They also contain glucarates, coumarins and other phenolic acids, terpenes and vitamin C. Its calcium is absorbed more efficiently than the calcium in milk (48).

Mustard oils: Contain compounds that break down into indoles and isothiocyanates during processing, cooking and chewing (5).

Nectarines: The carotenoid cryptoxanthin.

Nuts: Phytosterols, vitamin E, unsaturated fats.

Oats: Caffeic and ferulic acids, dietary fiber, phytic acid.

Okra: A good source of the carotenoids lutein and zeaxanthin; folic acid.

Olive oil: High in monounsaturated fats; alpha-tocopherol vitamin E, some carotenoids.

Onions: Quercetin and kaempferol (flavonols), organosulfides, glutathione. But white onions contain almost no quercetin.

Oranges: Along with other citrus fruits, rich in flavonoids, as well as the monoterpenes limonene and perillyl alcohol, cryptoxanthin. Also vitamin C, glucarates, mixed carotenoids, coumarins and other phenolic compounds and teriterpenes. Canned Mandarin oranges are especially rich in the carotenoid cryptoxanthin.

Orange peel: The oil is the most abundant source of limonene. Orange oil is 90% to 95% limonene by weight.

Papaya: Excellent source of the carotenoid cryptoxanthin and vitamin C.

Parsley: Flavones, rich in the carotenoids lutein and zeaxanthin, also beta carotene.

Parsnips: Phenolic compounds (especially flavonoids). Also carotenoids and terpenes.

Peaches, dried: Beta carotene and cryptoxanthin (another carotenoid). Peaches are a modest vitamin E source, as alpha-tocopherol.

Peanuts: Phytosterols, resveratrol.

Peas: Modest source of carotenoids; dietary fiber.

Pecans: Vitamin E.

Pistachio nuts: Rich in monounsaturated fat.

Potatoes: Vitamin C, the flavone aglycones (a plant phenol), glutathione. One study found the antioxidant activity of potatoes just a little below broccoli (50). Potato peel contains quercetin, chlorogenic acid and protease inhibitors, as well as dietary fiber.

Prunes: Caffeic and ferulic acids, fiber.

Pumpkin: Beta carotene, alpha carotene and other carotenoids, phenolic compounds.

Radishes: Protease inhibitors, flavonoids.

Romaine lettuce: A fair source of lutein and zeaxanthin, modest beta carotene.

Rosemary: Rosemary extract used in studies shows strong antioxidant properties, some of which may come from carnosol (51).

Rutabagas: A cruciferous vegetable. Rich in dithiolthiones, isothiocyanates, flavonoids and organosulfides. They also contain glucarates, coumarins and other phenolic compounds, and terpenes.

Safflower oil: Vitamin E (predominantly alpha-tocopherol with some gamma), phytosterols.

Sage: Monoterpenes.

Sesame seeds: Rich in phytosterols. Richest source of phytic acid.

Shallots: Organosulfides.

Soybeans (and soyfoods): Genistein and daidzein (isoflavonoids); particularly rich in saponins; other plant phenols such as flavonoids, coumarins, and caffeic and ferulic acid; lignans; terpenes; protease inhibitors; phytosterols; phytic acid (inositol hexaphosphate); dietary fiber. The oil is a non-fish source of essential fatty acids, from which omega-3s are derived. One of the richest sources in the American diet of gamma-tocopherol vitamin E because so many margarines, salad dressings and packaged baked goods rely on soybean oil. (Soyfoods include soy milk, tofu, tempeh and miso. Soy milk is made from pureed soybeans and water. Both tofu and tempeh are made from beans and grains.)

soy ploy

Soy flour is one of the most concentrated sources of soy protein. In most baked goods, you can substitute soy flour for up to a quarter of the wheat flour. Watch the cooking time: Soy flour browns a little more quickly than wheat flour.

Spearmint: Monoterpenes in the oil.

Spinach: Rich source of the carotenoids lutein and zeaxanthin; also a good beta carotene and vitamin C source. Modest source of alpha-tocopherol vitamin E. Protease inhibitors; folic acid. In one study, eating a lot of spinach or collard greens was associated with reduced risk of the leading cause of blindness over 65 (23).

Squash: Phenolic compounds. Winter squash is relatively high in beta carotene. Yellow squash and spaghetti squash are modest carotenoid sources.

Strawberries: Ellagic acid (which isn't well absorbed), moderately good source of the flavonols quercetin and kaempferol, vitamin C.

String beans: Modest source of the carotenoids lutein, zeaxanthin and beta carotene.

Sunflower seeds: Phytosterols. Very high in vitamin E (sunflower oil, too); the predominant form is alpha-tocopherol but also substantial gamma-tocopherol.

Sweet potatoes: Beta carotene, some vitamin E.

Swiss chard: Rich in the carotenoids lutein and zeaxanthin, a good source of beta carotene.

Tangerines: Flavonoids, coumarins and the carotenoid cryptoxanthin.

Tea: Green tea is a good source of phenolic compounds, including the flavonols quercetin and kaempferol. One subclass of flavonoid, catechins, accounts for up to 30% of the dry weight of green tea; the content of black tea depends on how it was processed. Also glucarates, coumarins. In one study, the antioxidant activity of both black and green teas was higher against one specific free radical than the activity of 22 vegetables. But they both showed pro-oxidant activity in the presence of copper (46).

Thyme: Rich in flavones.

Tomatoes: Rich source, along with tomato products, of the carotenoid lycopene, which gives tomatoes their red color. It is best absorbed from processed products, such as tomato sauce or paste, that are combined with a little oil. Vitamin C. Moderately good source of phenolic compounds (especially flavonoids), terpenes.

Turmeric: The yellow-colored spice contains curcumin (phenolic compound).

Turnips: A cruciferous vegetable. Rich in dithiolthiones, isothiocyanates, flavonoids and organosulfides. They also contain glucarates, coumarins and other phenolic compounds, and terpenes.

Turnip greens: Isothiocyanates and indoles. Rich source of the carotenoids lutein and zeaxanthin, plus beta carotene. The calcium in turnip greens is absorbed more effectively than from milk (48).

Vanilla bean: Vanillin, a phenolic acid.

Walnuts: Non-fish source of essential fatty acids, from which omega-3s are derived. Ellagic acid (not readily absorbed); vitamin E, phytosterols.

Watercress: A cruciferous vegetable rich in the carotenoids lutein and zeaxanthin. Also beta carotene, dithiolthiones, isothiocyanates, flavonoids and organosulfides. It also contains glucarates, coumarins and other phenolic compounds, and terpenes.

Watermelon: Lycopene, phenolic compounds.

Wheat: Phytic acid, dietary fiber, phytosterols.

Wheat germ: Vitamin E. Wheat germ oil is one of the richest sources of vitamin E. Also phytosterols.

Wild rice: Phytic acid.

Wine: Flavonoids, tannins (phenolic acids), resveratrol. Red wine is a good source of the flavonols quercetin and kaempferol.

primary sources

Steinmetz and Potter, "Vegetables, fruit, and cancer prevention: A review," Journal of the American Dietetic Association 1996; Dwyer, "Is There a Need to Change the American Diet?" presentation, "Dietary Phytochemicals in Cancer Prevention and Treatment," 1996; U.S. Department of Agriculture-National Cancer Institute Carotenoid Food Composition Data Base: Version I, 1993; Pennington: Bowes & Church's Food Values of Portions Commonly Used, 16th edition. For other sources, see Bibliography.

phytochemical glossary

Here is a list of terms used in phytochemical research.

Allium compounds: Another name for the organosulfides, or allyl sulfides, found in allium vegetables, which include garlic, onions, leeks, chives and shallots. Allium compounds such as diallyl sulfide and allyl methyl trisulfide may boost enzyme cancer detox systems and prevent bacteria from converting nitrates into substances that help make carcinogens. Garlic lowers cholesterol in people with elevated readings; diallyl sulfide is the suspected operative. Garlic also reduces blood clotting and lowers blood pressure. In addition to these and other possible health benefits, organosulfides give the allium family its pungency. But they may be lost in cooking.

Allyl methyl trisulfide: See "Allium compounds."

Alpha carotene: A powerful antioxidant carotenoid that the body converts to vitamin A, as needed. In population studies, alpha carotene is related to reduced risk of lung cancer. It may slow the proliferation of cancer cells. Carrots are a rich source.

Alpha tocopherol: The most common form of vitamin E, found both in the human body and in supplements. But gamma tocopherol is the primary source of vitamin E in the American diet, chiefly because so many foods such as margarine, salad dressings and packaged baked products are made with gamma-rich soybean oil.

Anthocyanins: Probably the most abundant flavonoid. See "Flavonoids."

Antioxidants: Antioxidants are chemical magnets that disarm highly reactive and damaging forms of oxygen, which are called collectively "free radicals." In chemicalspeak, these molecules are reactive because they have an extra electron to give away — and want to do it quick. Free radicals are the natural byproducts of energy metabolism in the cell but also come from outside sources. Although many phytochemicals are antioxidants, the most widely recognized and researched are beta carotene and vitamins C and E.

Beta carotene: A carotenoid that is stored in the liver, where the body converts it to vitamin A, as needed; found in dark, leafy greens and red, orange and yellow fruits and vegetables. A powerful antioxidant, beta carotene may play a role in slowing the progression of cancer. In population studies, it's related to decreased risk of lung cancer and oral can-

cers. It also may enhance immunity, help prevent cataracts and slow
plaque buildup in arteries. But it is not without controversy: In a study of
Finnish smokers, lung cancer increased among those taking supplements. Similar problems occurred in a study of former smokers, smokers
and workers exposed to asbestos. However, a 12-year U.S. trial of more
than 20,000 physicians, most of whom did not smoke, showed no such
increase nor any protective effect — for cancer or heart disease. These
findings don't negate beta carotene's promise, but they do complicate the
picture for now.

Biochanin A: See "Phytoesterogens."

Vitamin C: The most effective water-soluble antioxidant, especially
abundant in citrus fruits. Dr. Balz Frei, director of the Linus Pauling
Institute at Oregon State University, calls it the "first line of antioxidant
defense in human plasma." It works in concert with vitamin E to help
slow LDL oxidation, as well as protecting against some cancers. It also
protects parts of the eye against oxidative damage from ultraviolet light
and may prevent cataracts.

Caffeic and ferulic acids: Phenolic acids that in animal studies prevent
the formation of carcinogens in the stomach. Found in virtually all fruits
and vegetables.

Campesterol: See "Phytosterols."

Carcinogens: Cancer-causing substances.

Carnosol: An antioxidant phenolic compound in rosemary that may prevent cholesterol oxidation and prevent cancer. Rosemary extracts are
used in processed foods as a preservative, but flavor limits their application.

Carotenoids: A family of antioxidants that are also pigments in plants,
giving foods such as tomatoes, watermelon and sweet potatoes their
bright colors. Although more than 600 have been identified, only a handful are found in measurable quantities in the human body: alpha
carotene, beta carotene, lycopene, lutein, zeaxanthin and cryptoxanthin.
But around a dozen may be important. Carotenoids appear to play an
anticancer role and enhance immunity. Lycopene is increasingly gaining
ground as the most powerful antioxidant in the carotenoid family, particularly in relation to prostate and breast cancer. Two carotenoids found in
the eye, lutein and zeaxanthin, are believed to protect against the leading
cause of blindness in people over 65. Carotenoids also may play a role
in heart health: In LDL oxidation, antioxidants are consumed in a
sequence that begins with vitamin E; lycopene is next, followed by beta

names to know

Good sources of information on phytochemical developments include:

American Institute for Cancer Research Newsletter
(202-328-7744)

Environmental Nutrition Newsletter
(800-829-5384)

Tufts University Health & Nutrition Letter
(800-274-7581)

The University of California at Berkeley Wellness Letter
(904-445-6414)

carotene. Although carotenoids appear to be heat resistant, sunlight breaks them down in the presence of oxygen, so don't cut up vegetables and leave them out on the counter for a long time before using them. Cooking foods lightly makes their carotenoids more readily available.

Catechins: A subclass of flavonoids found in tea. Up to 30% of the dry weight of green tea leaves is catechins. Scientists believe catechins to be one of the important active substances that gives green tea extract its cancer-preventive and possibly curative properties in animal studies. But population studies show no such clear-cut protective effect.

Chalcones: See "Flavonoids."

Cholesterol: A important component of blood lipids (fats) manufactured by the liver that's also the precursor of the steroid hormones, such as the sex and "fight or flight" hormones. Too much of some kinds, specifically low-density lipoprotein (LDL) and very-low-density lipoprotein (VLDL), if oxidized, can collect inside artery walls as plaque, restricting blood flow, reducing vessel flexibility and leading to heart disease. High-density lipoprotein (HDL) helps move LDL cholesterol out of the system. Vitamin E, lycopene and beta carotene protect LDL from oxidation; their antioxidant activity is enhanced in the presence of vitamin C. People concerned with cholesterol should watch their intake of foods containing saturated fats, which stimulate the liver to make more cholesterol. Dietary cholesterol from animal-based foods has little effect on blood cholesterol in healthy people.

Coumarins: A class of widely occurring phenolic compounds, especially abundant in citrus fruits, that may help the enzymes that fend off cancer.

Cryptoxanthin: A carotenoid that's been associated with a decreased risk of cervical cancer. Abundant in many orange fruits, especially mango, tangerines, oranges and papaya.

Curcumin: A phenolic compound that gives turmeric and mustard spices their yellow color and exhibits anticancer, anti-inflammatory and antioxidant properties.

Diadzein: See "Genistein."

Diallyl sulfide: An allium compound that may have an anticancer role and is suspected of being the active ingredient in garlic that lowers cholesterol. See "Allium compounds."

Dithiolthiones: Organosulfur compounds that are abundant in cruciferous vegetables and may aid the enzymes that fend off carcinogens and other outside invaders. They also may inhibit the development of cancer.

Vitamin E: The most potent fat-soluble antioxidant, as well as one of the most widely recognized and researched. It occurs in eight chemical forms of varying potency; alpha tocopherol is the most common. But gamma tocopherol is the main type found in the American diet because so many products are made with soybean oil. Many kinds of research suggest that vitamin E works in concert with vitamin C, interfering with LDL oxidation and protecting against heart disease. But another part of this protection, its anticlotting function, may promote excessive bleeding in some people. Vitamin E also may play a role in immunity and in recovery from exercise-induced stress. In one study it delayed the onset of debilitating symptoms in Alzheimer's disease. It also shows anti-cancer promise. Getting enough E for such benefits from diet alone without overdoing fat is difficult because it's found primarily in oils, prompting many health experts to recommend taking supplements. Recommendations range from 100 to 800 IUs of vitamin E daily, with most in the 200 IUs to 400 IUs range, and some specify the natural form, d-alpha tocopherol, or mixed tocopherols. One study suggests that alpha and gamma tocopherol work in concert more effectively than indi-vidually against some particularly virulent free radicals. But the vitamin E research is far from definitive, and the supplement recommendations, controversial.

Ellagic acid: A phenolic acid with possible anticancer properties. Found in nuts, particularly walnuts, and fruits such as strawberries, cranberries and blackberries. But there is question as to its bioavailability (52).

Ferulic acid: See "Caffeic acid."

Fiber: Population studies suggest that a fiber-rich diet helps prevent both cancer and heart disease. Scientists suspect that one kind, insoluble fiber, prevents colon cancer in particular, possibly by increasing bulk and speeding waste through the colon, binding with carcinogens and produc-ing anticancer substances along the way. Whole wheat and wheat bran are rich sources. The second type, soluble fiber, appears to lower choles-terol and is abundant in oats, barley, legumes and vegetables such as potatoes. Most fruits, vegetables and grains contain a combination of the two types. Americans currently consume about 13 grams of fiber a day; the Daily Values on food labels, based on a 2,000-calorie diet, suggest 25 grams.

Flavanones: See "Flavonoids."

Flavonoids: A broad subcategory of plant phenolics (or phenolic compounds) made up of more than 4,000 compounds that are found in fruits, vegetables, wine and tea, especially green tea. "Plants have evolved to produce flavonoids to protect against fungal parasites, herbivores, pathogens and oxidative cell injury," writes Natalie Cook in a 1996 overview. "Conversely, flavonoids produce stimuli to assist in pollination and guide insects to their food source. For example, anthocyanins produce the pink, red, mauve, violet and blue colors of flowers, fruits and vegetables." The many potential effects of flavonoids include defending cells against carcinogens, curbing the oxidation of LDL cholesterol and preventing blood clotting. Major flavonoid classes include flavonols, flavanones, catechins, anthocyanins, isoflavones, dihydroflavonols and chalcones.

Flavonols: See "Flavonoids" and "Quercetin."

Folic acid: In the realm of cancer study, a deficiency of this nutrient may lead to chromosome and/or DNA damage that can open the way for cancer. In heart research, low folate causes high levels of homocysteine in the blood, which increases the risk for stroke and heart attack. Found in dark leafy greens.

Free radicals: Highly reactive molecular byproducts of energy metabolism that can damage cells and DNA. Free radicals also come from environmental sources such as cigarette smoke, auto and industrial emissions and sunlight. A leading theory of aging holds that free radicals are largely responsible for the declines and diseases associated with aging.

Genistein: An isoflavone, like daidzein, uniquely abundant in soyfoods; some of it is converted in the intestines to a compound that acts as a weak estrogen (phytoestrogen); the subject of hundreds of studies. Scientists believe it may be a significant anticancer force, particularly with hormone-related cancers such as breast cancer. It also may offer protection against cardiovascular disease by reducing blood clotting and/or cholesterol levels. Further, it may play a role in bone health and in relieving menopausal symptoms. See "Phytoestrogens."

Glutathione: A water-soluble antioxidant found in onions and potatoes that may detoxify cancer-causing substances. It also supports the actions of other antioxidants, such as vitamins C and E and beta carotene.

HDL cholesterol: See "Cholesterol."

Indole-3-carbinol: See "Indoles."

Indoles: Found in cruciferous vegetables, indoles may prevent carcinogens from reaching their intended goal inside of cells. They're formed from glucosinolates, which are particularly abundant in brussels sprouts, rutabaga and mustard greens. One, indole-3-carbinol, may help protect against estrogen-related cancers, such as breast cancer.

Inositol hexaphosphate: See "Phytic acid."

Isoflavones: Genistein and daidzein are the most prominent; found almost exclusively in soybeans and soyfoods; some are converted in the intestine to compounds with estrogen-mimicking functions; may help prevent hormone-related cancers, such as breast cancer. Sometimes scientists will refer to foods as "containing isoflavones" as a kind of shorthand. See "Genistein."

Isothiocyanates: Among the most effective cancer-prevention agents known. These organosulfur compounds boost the cancer-fighting power of certain enzymes. One, sulphorophane, appears to be especially potent. They are partially responsible for the pungency of some cruciferous vegetables.

Kaempferol: A flavonoid, like quercetin, found broadly in fruits and vegetables.

LDL cholesterol: See "Cholesterol" and "Oxidation."

Lignans (also called phenolic lignans): Plant phenolics converted in the intestines to a type of phytoestrogen ("plant" estrogen) with antioxidant properties. As a weak estrogen, lignans may affect hormone-related cancers by tying up the estrogen receptors on cells. Lignans are abundant in flax seed and flour, whole grain products and some berries. Vegetables and other grains are also sources.

Limonene: This monoterpene, which shows so much promise for cancer treatment, is the same substance that gives lemon scent to furniture polish and grease-cutting power to detergent. (One scientist once described how it dissolved a researcher's plastic pipette.) It is found in citrus oils, as well as garlic and the oils of other plants; it is used in Japan to dissolve gallstones. Limonene and its chemical cousin, perillyl alcohol, show powerful anticancer effects in animals. In rats, limonene caused the complete regression of mammary tumors. Human studies are underway with cancer patients.

Lutein: A powerful antioxidant and one of two carotenoids found in the eye. These yellow pigments are believed to filter out harmful blue light and protect against age-related macular degeneration, the leading cause of blindness in people over 65. Studies show that eating lots of spinach

and collard greens — rich in lutein and its carotenoid partner, zeaxanthin — may substantially lower the risk of this irreversible disease. More resistant to cooking than other carotenoids, it's also associated with decreased lung cancer risk.

Lycopene: Emerging as the most powerful antioxidant of the carotenoid family. The pigment gives tomatoes their red color and also makes grapefruit and watermelon pink. The most concentrated carotenoid in the prostate, lycopene is linked to reduced prostate cancer risk in population studies. In one study, it inhibited cancer cell proliferation more effectively than alpha carotene or beta carotene. It is also stirring interest as a possible breast cancer preventative.

Monoterpenes: A broad category of compounds that may prevent, slow and/or reverse the progression of some cancers as well as affect blood clotting and cholesterol. The two most notable are limonene and perillyl alcohol. Found in the essential oils of citrus fruits, cherries, spearmint and dill.

Monounsaturated fats: Especially abundant in olive oil and canola oil. Monounsaturated fats slightly lower total cholesterol; this action may be due to their phytosterols.

Nitrates, nitrites: Nitrosamines are known to cause cancer. Nitrites in smoked and fermented foods and nitrates, found naturally in some foods and changed to nitrites by bacteria in the mouth, combine with amines in the stomach as protein breaks down to form nitrosamines. Vitamins C and E and phenolic compounds, such as quercetin, block this reaction in the stomach and may thus prevent cancer. Nitrates and nitrites are also found in some cured meats.

Organosulfides: The mostly smelly compounds in the allium (onion-garlic) and cruciferous (broccoli-kale) families. Dithiolthiones, including sulforophane, and indoles are the dominant ones in the cruciferous vegetables; they work primarily against cancer. Allium compounds such as diallyl sulfide are operative in the allium vegetables, especially garlic; they have a variety of anticancer and heart health functions.

Oxidation: Occurs when something is chemically united with certain types of oxygen with the help of an oxidizing agent. Combustion — fire — is the result of oxidation. It also occurs when metals rust or cut apples or potatoes turn brown. (Squeezing lemon juice on apples to prevent discoloration is an example of an antioxidant in action.) In the body, highly reactive free radical forms of oxygen grab onto other compounds in cells, causing structural damage to cell protein or fats or to the DNA within the nucleus. Polyunsaturated fat molecules in cell membranes and LDL cholesterol are particularly susceptible to free radical damage. Oxidized LDL cholesterol changes readily into substances that contribute to lesions in blood vessel walls, building up as plaque that gradually shrinks the circumference of the vessels and makes them less flexible.

Perillyl Alcohol: The limonene cousin that has been shown in animal studies to shrink tumors in animals, including stubborn pancreatic tumors. Found in citrus oils, this monterpene is being tested on humans. The intervention trials are using amounts far greater than what is ordinarily consumed from fruits and vegetables.

Phenolic compounds (or plant phenols): A broad category of antioxidant compounds that includes flavonoids, phenolic acids (which includes ellagic acid, tannic acid and vanillin) and hydroxycinnamic acid derivatives (caffeic, chlorogenic and ferulic acids, curcumin, coumarins). Lignans are another class of phenolic compounds. Found in almost all fruits, vegetables and grains, phenolic compounds affect the quality, appeal and stability of foods with antioxidant action, flavor and color. They give wine its characteristic hues, flavors and astringency. Besides scavenging for free radicals, some phenolic compounds appear to interrupt cancer development in other ways. Some also hinder LDL oxidation. It's not yet known how well plant phenols are absorbed from foods.

Phytic acid (inositol hexaphosphate): A heat- and acid-stable phytate in cereal grains, nuts and seeds, especially abundant in sesame seeds and soybeans. Although a high-fiber diet is thought to protect against some cancers, the argument has been advanced that phytic acid, not fiber, may provide the protection. It appears to slow the formation of cancer in lab and animal studies. It also may help control blood sugar, cholesterol and triglycerides.

Phytoestrogens: So-called "plant" estrogens that are produced in the intestines from certain flavonoids, isoflavones (most notably genistein, biochanin A and daidzein) and lignans. Often scientists simply say foods "contain" isoflavones as a kind of shorthand. Phytoestrogens are 250 to 1,000 times weaker than human estrogen but still impact the body. They are suspected of blocking estrogens by tying up estrogen receptors on cells, thus affecting hormone-related cancers, including breast and prostate cancer. They also may decrease hot flashes and other symptoms of menopause, although most of the evidence is anecdotal so far. One scientist likens phytoestrogens to a key that can fit a lock but not open it, effectively blocking the real key. Some phytoestrogens are similar to tamoxifen, a drug used to treat some breast cancers. Soyfoods are rich sources. In one study, tofu was found to contain the most isoflavones of the foods tested, though amount varied by brand (53).

Phytosterols: Plant sterols that in modest amounts can lower cholesterol and that show anticancer activity in lab and animal studies. Nuts (almonds, cashews, peanuts), seeds (sesame, sunflower), whole wheat, corn, soybeans and many vegetable oils are good sources. Some scientists speculate that phytosterols are responsible for the cholesterol-lowering properties of mono- and polyunsaturated oils. Some key sterols that lower cholesterol are beta-sitosterol, stigmasterol and campesterol.

Polyunsaturated fats: Like monounsaturated fats, polyunsaturated fats lower cholesterol. Two groups of polyunsaturated fats, omega-3s and omega-6s, are essential fatty acids, which the body requires but cannot manufacture. Omega-6s are in seeds and in vegetable and seed oils. Omega-3s are in green leafy vegetables, canola oil and soybeans. In slightly different form, omega-3s are found in fish and especially concentrated in cold-water fish such as salmon, trout, sardines and mackerel. (The source of these plant substances in fish are plankton and algae.) Because omega-3s and omega-6s compete for the same enzymes in the body, excessive intake of omega-6 can lead to a relative omega-3 deficiency.

Pro-oxidant: Any chemical compound that enhances oxidation. Under some conditions, some phytochemicals have been shown to act as pro-oxidants, one reason scientists wave people off supplements. Americans often assume — wrongly — that if a little of something is good, a lot must be better. If you're talking spinach, you probably can't (or won't) eat too much; if you're talking milligrams of sulphorophane in a capsule, you might do harm. With the exception of vitamin E, too little is known about most phytochemicals to mega-dose.

Protease inhibitors: Proteins that are plentiful in plants. Lab and animal studies show that they may aid DNA repair, which can slow cancer cell division and help return a cell to its normal state. They also may prevent tumors from releasing proteases that destroy neighboring cells. Found especially in soyfoods, also seeds and legumes.

Quercetin: The most studied flavonoid because it is among the most abundant; a more potent antioxidant than vitamin E, according to some research. Onions are the richest source; it's also found in wine and tea. (Many sources say "onions, tea, wine and apples" because these were the main dietary sources in a major Netherlands study.) Among other functions, it may block carcinogens as well as slow the growth and spread of cancer cells. It also may prevent the conversion of nitrites in the stomach to compounds that become building blocks for carcinogens. Quercetin appears to survive the heat of cooking, and about 5% to 10% of the quercetin from onions is absorbed by the body.

Resveratrol: A naturally occuring phenolic fungicide in grapes (and wine) that may that protect the heart. Peanuts also contain resveratrol.

Retinol: Another name for vitamin A. See "Carotenoids."

Saponins: Naturally occurring compounds found in most vegetables and herbs, but especially abundant in soybeans and other beans and legumes. Lab and animal research with saponins suggests they may prevent cancer cells from multiplying. They may also help control blood sugar, cholesterol and triglycerides.

Selenium: A trace mineral that may alter the course of cancer by helping certain enzymes protect cells against damage. The amount found in produce is directly related to the amount in the soil where it is grown, and selenium is readily taken up by the body. Its antioxidant function may prevent premature aging. Garlic contains selenium, and one scientist has used enriched soil to increase the amount in garlic bulbs.

Silymarin: A flavonoid present in artichokes that has been used in Europe to treat alcohol-related liver diseases. This strong antioxidant protects against liver toxicity in animals and plays a cancer-protective role.

Sitosterol (beta-sitosterol): See "Phytosterols."

Stigmasterol: See "Phytosterols."

Sulphorophane: See "Isothiocyanates."

Terpenes: Monoterpenes and triterpenes comprise the terpenes under investigation. Most of the attention is focused on two monoterpenes: limonene and perillyl alcohol.

Vanillin: A phenolic compound in vanilla beans and cloves.

Zeaxanthin: A strong antioxidant and one of two yellow carotenoids found in the eye that are believed to filter out harmful blue light and protect against age-related macular degeneration, the leading cause of blindness in people over 65. Studies show that eating lots of spinach and collard greens — rich in zeaxanthin and its carotenoid partner, lutein — may substantially lower the risk for this irreversible condition. Also in the eye, the antioxidants may help scavenge free radicals caused by exposure to sunlight. Zeazanthin is also associated with decreased lung cancer risk. Corn and eggs are also good sources.

bibliography
footnote references

The Science Behind the Recipes contains specific references to the following sources:

1. **Willett, W.C., et al.** Mediterranean diet pyramid: a cultural model for healthy eating. *Am J Clin Nutr* (1995):61(suppl):1402S-1406S.

2. **Giovannucci, E., et al.** Intake of carotenoids and retinol in relation to risk of prostate cancer. *J Natl Cancer Instit* (1995);87:1767-1776.

3. **Symposium: "Tomatoes and Health."** Transcript of tomato health panel hosted by the California Tomato Growers Association, Inc. Feb. 1997, Sacramento, CA.

4. **U.S. Department of Agriculture-National Cancer Institute Carotenoid Food Composition Data Base:** Version I, 1993.

5. **Dietary Phytochemicals in Cancer Prevention and Treatment.** Proceedings of the American Institute for Cancer Research's sixth annual research conference. Aug. 31-Sept. 1, 1995, Washington, D.C.

6. **Perrig, W.J., et al.** The relation between antioxidants and memory performance in the old and the very old. *J Am Geriat Soc* (1997);45:718-724.

7. **Pandey, D.K., et al.** Dietary vitamin C and beta-carotene and risk of death in middle-aged men — The Western Electric Study. *Am J Epidemiol* (1995);142:1269-1278.

8. **Riemersma, R.A.** Epidemiology and the role of antioxidants in preventing coronary heart disease: a brief overview. *Proc Nutr Soc* (1994);53:59-65.

9. **Meydani, S.N., et al.** Vitamin E supplementation and in vivo immune response in healthy elderly subjects. *JAMA* (1997);277:1380-1386.

10. **Steinmetz, K.A., and Potter, J.D.** Vegetables, fruit and cancer prevention: a review. *J Am Diet Assoc* (1996);96:1027-1039.

11. **Albanes, D. et al.** Alpha-Tocopherol, Beta Carotene Cancer Prevention Study Group. The effect of vitamin E and beta carotene on the incidence of lung cancer and other cancers in male smokers. *N Engl J Med* (1994);330:1029-1035.

12. **Omenn, G.S.** Beta carotene and retinol efficacy trial (CARET) *N Engl J Med* (1996);334:1150-1155.

13. **Bloch, A., and Thomson, C.A.** Position of the American Dietetic Association: phytochemicals and functional foods. *J Am Diet Assoc* (1995);95:493-496.

14. **Hennekens, C., et al.** Lack of effect of long-term supplementation with beta-carotene on the incidence of malignant neoplasms and cardiovascular disease. *N Engl J Med* (1996);334:1145-1149.

15. **Bohm, F.** Carotenoids enhance vitamin E antioxidant efficiency. *J Am Chem Soc* (1997).

16. **Bender, D.A., and Bender, A.E.,** *Nutrition — A Reference Handbook.* Oxford Univ Press; New York, 1997.

17. **VERIS Presentation Abstracts** from the United Nations and World Health Organization First Joint Conference on Healthy Aging, April 29- May 1, 1996.

18. Esterbauer, H., et al. Role of vitamin E in preventing the oxidation of low-density lipoprotein. *Am J Clin Nutr* (1991);53:314S-321S.

19. Frei, B. Reactive oxygen species and antioxidant vitamins: mechanisms of action. *Am J Med* (1994);97(suppl)3A;5S-12S.

20. Sano, M., et al. A controlled trial of selegiline, alpha-tocopherol, or both as treatment for Alzheimer's disease. *N Engl J Med* (1997);336:1216-1222.

21. VERIS Research Summary. The role of antioxidants in skin care and protection. May 1997.

22. VERIS Research Information Service. *Carotenoids Fact Book,* 1996.

23. Seddon, J.M., et al. Dietary carotenoids, vitamins A, C, and E, and advanced age-related macular degeneration. *JAMA* (1994); 272:1413-1420.

24. Taylor, A., et al. Relations among aging, antioxidant status, and cataract. *Am J Clin Nutr* (1995);62(suppl):1439S-1447S.

25. Robertson, J.M., et al. A possible role for vitamins C and E in cataract prevention. *Am J Clin Nutr* (1991);53:346S-351S.

26. VERIS Vitamin E Research Summary. Potential beneficial role of antioxidants in HIV infection and AIDS. May 1995.

27. Weindruch, R. Caloric restriction and aging. *Scientific American* (1996);Jan:46-52.

28. American Cancer Society Advisory Committee Guidelines on Diet, Nutrition and Cancer Prevention (1996).

29. Dorant, E., et al. Consumption of onions and a reduced risk of stomach carcinoma. *Gastroenterology* (1996);110;12-20.

30. Yang, C.S. Tea and cancer: a review. *J Natl Cancer Inst* (1993);85:1038-1049.

31. Bates, C.J. Vitamin A. *Lancet* (1995);345:31-35.

32. Dietary Phytochemicals in Cancer Prevention and Treatment. American Institute for Cancer Research's sixth annual research conference. Aug. 31-Sept. 1, 1995, Washington, D.C.

33. The American Heart Association's death rate tables, (1995).

34. Messina, M., and Messina, V. *The Simple Soybean and Your Health.* Avery Publishing Group, NY, 1994.

35. Demrow, H.S., et al. Administration of wine and grape juice inhibits in vivo platelet activity and thrombosis in stenosed canine coronary arteries. *Circulation* (1995);91:1182-1188.

36. Hertog, M.G.L., et al. Flavonoid intake and long term risk of coronary heart disease and cancer in the Seven Countries Study. *Arch Intern Med* (1995);155:381-386.

37. Hennekens, C., et al. Discussion. *Am J Med* (1994);97(suppl3A):22S-28S.

38. Jialal, I. University of Texas Southwestern Medical Center at Dallas. Personal communication, 1997.

39. Christen, S., et al. Gamma-tocopherol traps mutagenic electrophiles such as NOx and complements alpha-tocopherol: physiological implications. *Proc Natl Acad Sci* (1997);94:3217-3222.

40. Howard, B.V., and Kritchevsky, D. Phytochemicals and cardiovascular disease: a statement for healthcare professionals from the American Heart Association. *Circulation* (1997);95:2591-2593.

41. Rokitzki, L., et al. Alpha tocopherol supplementation in racing cyclists during extreme endurance training (abstract). *I J Sport Nutr* (1994);4:253-264.

42. Rokitzki, L., et al. Lipid peroxidation and antioxidant vitamins under extreme endurance stress (abstract). *Acta Physiologica Scandinavica* (1994);151:149-158.

43. Cook, N.C., and Samman, S. Flavonoids — chemistry, metabolism, cardioprotective effects and dietary sources. *Nutr Biochem* (1996);7:66-76.

44. Gilman, M.W., et al. Protective effective of fruits and vegetables on development of stroke in men. *JAMA* (1995);273:1113-1117.

45. Appel, L.J., et al. A clinical trial of the effects of dietary patterns on blood pressure. *N Engl J Med* (1997);336:1117-1124.

46. Cao, G., et al., Antioxidant capacity of tea and common vegetables. *J Agric Food Chem* (1996); 44:3426-3431.

47. Deneo-Pellegrini, H., et al. Vegetables, fruits, and risk of colorectal cancer: a case-control study from Uruguay. *Nutr Cancer* (1996); 25:297-303.

48. Weaver, C.M., and Plawecki, K.L. Dietary calcium: adequacy of a vegetarian diet. *Am J Clin Nutr* (1994);59(suppl):1238S-1241S.

49. Sabaté, J., and Fraser, G.E. Nuts: a new protective food against coronary heart disease. *Current Opinion in Lipidology* (1994);5:11-16.

50. Al-Saikhan, M.S., et al. Antioxidant activity and total phenolics in different genotypes of potato (Solanum tuberosum, L). *J Food Sci* (1995);60:341-347.

51. Huang, M., et al. Inhibition of skin tumorigenesis by rosemary and its constituents carnosol and ursolic acid. *Cancer Res* (1994); 54:701-708.

52. Stoner, G. Ohio State University in Columbus, Dept. of Preventive Medicine. Personal communication, 1997.

53. Dwyer, J.T., et al. Tofu and soy drinks contain phytoestrogens. *J Am Diet Assoc* (1994);94:739-743.

general references

The following sources provided information used in the preparation of this book.

Abbey, M., et al. Partial replacement of saturated fatty acids with almonds or walnuts lowers total plasma cholesterol and low-density-lipoprotein cholesterol. *Am J Clin Nutr* (1994);59:995-999.

Albanes, D., et al. Effects of alpha-tocopherol and beta-carotene supplements on cancer incidence in the Alpha-Tocopherol Beta-Carotene Cancer Prevention Study. *Am J Clin Nutr* (1995);62(suppl):1427S-1430S.

American Council on Science and Health. *Special Report: Dietary Fiber* (1997).

Anderson, J.W., et al. Meta-analysis of the effects of soy protein intake on serum lipids. *N Engl J Med* (1995);333:276-282.

Beecher, C.W.W. Cancer preventive properties of varieties of *Brassica oleracea*: a review. *Am J Clin Nutr* (1994);59:1166S-1170S.

Bendich, A. Biological functions of dietary carotenoids. *Ann NY Acad Sci* (1993);61-67.

Blonz, E. *Your Personal Nutritionist: Antioxidant Counter.* Signet Books, 1996.

Blumberg, J. Are antioxidants at an awkward age? *J Am Coll Nutr* (1994);13:218-219.

Caragay, A. Cancer-preventative foods and ingredients. *Food Tech* (1992);April:65-68.

Christen, W.G. Antioxidants and eye disease. *Am J Med* (1994);97(suppl3A):14S-17S.

Chug-Ahuja, J.K., et al. The development and application of a carotenoid database for fruits, vegetables, and selected multicomponent foods. *J Am Diet Assoc* (1993);93:318-323.

Collins, A., et al. Micronutrients and oxidative stress in the aetiology of cancer. *Proc Nut Soc* (1994);53:67-75.

Conner, W.E. Omega-3 essential fatty acids in infant neurological development. *Pufa Information Backgrounder*, Hoffman-La Roche, 1996.

Constantinou, A., et al. The dietary anticancer agent ellagic acid is a potent inhibitor of DNA topoisomerases in vitro. *Nutr Cancer* (1995);23:121-130.

Coodley, G.O., et al. Beta-carotene in HIV infection. *Ann NY Acad Sci* (1993);277-278.

Dausch, J.G., and Nixon, D.W. Garlic: a review of its relationship to malignant disease. *Prev Med* (1990);19:346-361.

Decker, E.A. The role of phenolics, conjugated linoleic acid, carnosine and pyrroloquinoline quinone as nonessential dietary antioxidants. *Nut Rev* (1995); 53:49-58.

de Lorgeril, M., et al. Mediterranean alpha-linolenic acid-rich diet in secondary prevention of coronary heart disease. *Lancet* (1994);343:1454-1459.

de Lorgeril, M., et al. Effect of a Mediterranean type diet on the rate of cardiovascular complications in patients with coronary artery disease. *JACC* (1996); 28:1103-1108.

Devaraj, S., et al. The effects of alpha tocopherol supplementation on monocyte function. *J Clin Invest* (1996);98:1-8.

Di Mascio, P., et. al. Antioxidant defense systems: the role of carotenoids, tocopherols, and thiols. *Am J Clin Nut* (1991);53:194S-200S.

Dorant, E., et al. Garlic and its significance for the prevention of cancer in humans: a critical view. *Br J Cancer* (1993);67:424-429.

Dragsted, L.O., et al. Cancer-protective factors in fruits and vegetables: biochemical and biological background. *Pharma Toxicol* (1993);72(suppl1):116-135.

Drewnowski, A., et al. Diet quality and dietary diversity in France: implications for the French Paradox. *J Am Diet Assoc* (1996);96:663-669.

Eastman, P. "Phytamins" are not ready for public consumption (news section). *J Natl Cancer I* (1995);87:1430-1432.

Fielding, R. Does diet or alcohol explain the French paradox? *Lancet* (1995); 345;527-528.

Franceschi, S., et al. Tomatoes and risk of digestive tract cancers. *Int J Cancer* (1994);59:181-184.

Frankel, E.N., et al. Inhibition of oxidation of human low-density lipoprotein by phenolic substances in red wine. *Lancet* (1993);341:454-457.

Fraser, G.E. Diet and coronary heart disease: beyond dietary fats and low-density-lipoprotein cholesterol. *Am J Clin Nutr* (1994);59(suppl):1117S-1123S.

Fuhrman, B., et al. Consumption of red wine with meals reduces the susceptibility of human plasma and low-density lipoprotein to lipid peroxidation. *Am J Clin Nutr* (1995);61:549-554.

Fujiki, H., et al. Japanese green tea as a cancer preventive in humans. *Nut Review* (1996);54:S67-S70.

Gaziano, J.M. Antioxidant vitamins and coronary artery disease risk. *Am J Med* (1994);97(suppl3A):18S-21S.

Gelb, M.H., et al. The inhibition of protein prenyltransferases by oxygenated metabolites of limonene and perillyl alcohol. *Cancer Lett* (1995);91:169-175.

Goldbohm, R.A., et al. Consumption of black tea and cancer risk: a prospective cohort study. *J Natl Cancer Inst* (1996);88:93-100.

Goldfarb, A.H. Antioxidants: role of supplementation to prevent exercise-induced oxidative stress. *Med Sci Sports Exerc* (1993);25:232-236.

Gooderham, M.J., et al. A soy protein isolate rich in genistein and daidzein and its effects on plasma isoflavone concentrations, platelet aggregation, blood lipids and fatty acid composition of plasma phospholipid in normal men. *J Nutr* (1996);126:2000-2006.

Gould, M.N., et al. Chemoprevention and therapy of cancer by d-limonene. *Critical Rev Oncongenesis* (1994);5:1-22.

Gould, M.N. Prevention and therapy of mammary cancer by monoterpenes. *J Cell Biochem* (1995);S22:139-144.

Graf, E., and Eaton, J. Suppression of colonic cancer by dietary phytic acid. *Nutr Cancer* (1993);19:11-19.

Greenberg, E.R., et al. A clinical trial of antioxidant vitamins to prevent colorectal adenoma. *N Eng J Med* (1994);331:141-147.

Greenberg, E.R., et al. Mortality associated with low plasma concentration of beta carotene and the effect of oral supplementation. *JAMA* (1996);275:699-703.

Hasegawa, T. Anti-stress effect of beta carotene. *Ann NY Acad Sci* (1993);281-283.

Helzlsouer, K.J., et al. Prospective study of serum micronutrients and ovarian cancer. *J Natl Cancer Inst* (1996);88:32-37.

Hennekens, C. Antioxidant vitamins and cancer. *Am J Med* (1994); 97(suppl3A):2S-4S.

Herbert, V. Commentary: the antioxidant supplement myth. *Am J Clin Nutr* (1994):60:157-158.

Herbert, V. Symposium: pro-oxidant effects of antioxidant vitamins. *J Nutr* (1996);126:1197S-1200S.

Herbert, V. The value of antioxidant supplements vs. their natural counterparts. *J Am Diet Assoc* (1997);97:375-376.

Hertog, M.G.L., and Hollman, P.C.H. Potential health effects of the dietary flavonol quercetin (abstract). *Euro J Clin Nut* (1996);50:63-72.

Hertog, M.G.L., et al. Flavonoid content of vegetables and fruits commonly consumed in the Netherlands. *J Agri Food Chem* (1992);40:2379-2383.

Hertog, M.G.L., et al. Content of potentially anticarcinogenic flavonoids of tea infusions, wines, and fruit juices. *J Agric Food Chem* (1993);41:1242-1246.

Kanter, M.M., et al. Effects of an antioxidant vitamin mixture on lipid peroxidation at rest and postexercise. *J Appl Physiol* (1993);74:965-969.

Khachik, F., et al. Effect of food preparation on qualitative and quantitative distribution of major carotenoid constituents of tomatoes and several green vegetables. *J Agric Food Chem* (1992);40:390-398.

Kleijnen, J., et al. Garlic, onions and cardiovascular risk factors. A review of the evidence from human experiments with emphasis on commercially available preparations. *Br J Clin Pharmac* (1989);28:535-544.

Kushi, L.H., et al. Health implications of Mediterranean diets in light of contemporary knowledge. 1. Plant foods and dairy products. *Am J Clin Nutr* (1995):61(suppl):1407S-1415S.

Kushi, L.H., et al. Health implications of Mediterranean diets in light of contemporary knowledge. 2. Meat, wine, fats, and oils. *Am J Clin Nutr* (1995):61(suppl):1416S-1427S.

Lawson, T., et al. Isolation of compounds with antimutagenic activity from Savory Chieftain cabbage. *J Agric Food Chem* (1989);37:1363-1367.

Lehman, J., et al. Vitamin E in foods from high and low linoleic acid diets. *J Am Diet Assoc* (1986);86:1208-1216.

Le Marchand, L., et al. Vegetable and fruit consumption in relation to prostate cancer risk in Hawaii: a reevaluation of the effect of dietary beta-carotene. *Am J Epidemiol* (1991);133:215-219.

Levy, J., et al. Lycopene is a more potent inhibitor of human cancer cell proliferation than either alpha-carotene or beta-carotene. *Nutr Cancer* (1995);24:257-266.

Mangels, A.R., et al. Carotenoid content of fruits and vegetables: an evaluation of analytic data. *J Am Diet Assoc* (1993);93:284-296.

Manson, J.E., et al. Antioxidants and cardiovascular disease: a review. *J Am Coll Nutr* (1993);12:426-432.

Margen, S., and editors of University of California at Berkeley Wellness Letter. *The Wellness Encyclopedia of Food and Nutrition* (1992).

Marlett, J.A. Content and composition of dietary fiber in 117 frequently consumed foods. *J Am Diet Assoc* (1992):175-180.

Mares-Perlman, J.A. Serum antioxidants and age-related macular degeneration in a population-based case-control study. *Arch Ophthalmol* (1995);113:1518-1523.

McClinton-Adams, J.L., et al. Cancer prevention with beta carotene. *Ann Pharmacotheraphy* (1994);28.

McNamee, D. Limonene trial in cancer. *Lancet (*1993);342:801.

Messina, M. and Messina, V. Increasing use of soyfoods and their potential role in cancer prevention. *J Am Diet Assoc* (1991);91:836-840.

Messina, M. Highlights of the second international symposium on the role of soy in preventing and treating chronic disease. The Soy Connection (1997); 5.

Meydani, M., et al. Protective effect of vitamin E on exercise-induced oxidative damage in young and older adults. *Am J Physiol* (1993);64:R992-R998.

Micozzi, M.S., et al. Carotenoid analyses of selected raw and cooked foods associated with a lower risk of cancer. *J Natl Cancer Inst* (1990);82:282-285.

Morris, D. L., et al. Serum carotenoids and coronary heart disease; the Lipid Research Clinics Coronary Primary Prevention Trial and Follow-up Study. *JAMA* (1994);272:1439-1441.

Negri, E., et al. Intake of selected micronutrients and the risk of breast cancer. *Int J Cancer* (1996);65:140-144.

Pietinen, P., et al. Intake of dietary fiber and risk of coronary heart disease in a cohort of Finnish men, the Alpha-Tocopherol, Beta-Carotene Cancer Prevention Study. *Circulation* (1996);94:2720-2727.

Pike, L. Vegetable Improvement Center, Texas A&M University. Personal communication, 1997.

Prabhala, R.H., et al. Influence of beta-carotene on immune functions. *Ann NY Acad Sci* (1993);262-263.

Reddy, B.S., et al. Chemoprevention of colon cancer by organoselenium compounds and impact of high- or low-fat diets. *J Natl Cancer Inst* (1997);89:506-511.

Renaud, S., et al. Cretan Mediterranean diet for prevention of coronary heart disease. *Am J Clin Nutr* (1995);61(suppl):1360S-1367S.

Reynolds, R.D. Vitamin supplements: current controversies. *J Am Coll Nutr* (1994); 13:118-126.

Rimm, E.B., and Ellison, R.C. Alcohol in the Mediterranean diet. *Am J Clin Nutr* (1995);61(suppl):1378S-1382S.

Rimm, E.B., et al. Review of moderate alcohol consumption and reduced risk of coronary heart disease: is the effect due to beer, wine or spirits? *BMJ* (1996);312:731-736.

Rimm, E.B., et al. Vegetable, fruit, and cereal fiber intake and risk of coronary heart disease among men. *JAMA* (1996);275:447-451.

Rimm, E.B., et al. Relation between intake of flavonoids and risk for coronary heart disease in male health professionals. *Ann Intern Med* (1996);125:384-389.

Robertson, J.M., et al. A possible role for vitamins C and E in cataract prevention. *Am J Clin Nutr* (1991);53:346S-351S.

Rosenberg, I.H. Nutrient requirements for optimal health: what does that mean? *J Nutr* (1994);124(suppl);1777S-1779S.

Ross, A.C., and Ternus, M.E. Vitamin A as a hormone: recent advances in understanding the actions of retinol, retinoic acid and beta carotene. *J Am Diet Assoc* (1993);93:1285-1290.

Sabaté, J., and Fraser, G.E. The probable role of nuts in preventing coronary heart disease. *Primary Cardiology* (1993);19:65-72.

Sabaté, J. Does nut consumption protect against ischaemic heart disease? *European J Clin Nut* (1993);47(suppl1):S71-S75.

Schiffman, S.S., and Warwick, Z.S. Effect of flavor enhancement of foods for the elderly on nutritional status: food intake, biochemical indices, and anthropometric measures. *Physiology & Behavior* (1993);55:395-402.

Schoenfeld, E.R., et al. Recent epidemiologic studies on nutrition and cataract in India, Italy and the United States. *J Am Coll Nutr* (1993);12:521-526.

Schroeder, D.J., et al. Cancer prevention with beta carotene. *Annl Pharmac* (1994);28:470-472.

Schwartz, J.L., et al. The dual roles of nutrients as antioxidants and pro-oxidants: their effects on tumor growth. *J Nutr* (1996);126:1221S-1227S.

Seddon, J.M., et al. The use of vitamin supplements and the risk of cataract among U.S. male physicians. *Am J of Pub Health* (1994);84:788-792.

Sies, H. and Krinsky, N.I. The present status of antioxidant vitamins and beta- carotene. *Am J Clin Nutr* (1995);62(suppl):1299S-1300S.

Simopoulos, A.P. The Mediterranean food guide: Greek column rather than an Egyptian pyramid. *Nut Today* (1995);30:54-61.

Slavin, J.L. Whole grains and health: separating the wheat from the chaff. *Nut Today* (1994):29;6-11.

Soy Connection, The. Researchers from around the world present on a wide range of chronic diseases. 1997;5:1-4.

Sperduto, R.D., et al. The Linxian cataract studies. Two nutrition intervention trials. *Arch Opthalmol* (1993);111:1246-1253.

Spiller, G.A. Health effects of Mediterranean diets and monounsaturated fats. Presented at the 75th AACC Annual Meeting, 1990. *CFW Review* (1991);36:812-814.

Spiller, G. A., et al. Effect of a diet high in monounsaturated fat from almonds on plasma cholesterol and lipoproteins. *J Am Coll Nutr* (1992);11:126-130.

Steinmetz, K.A. and Potter, J.D. Vegetables, fruit and cancer. I. Epidemiology. *Cancer Causes and Control* (1991); 2:325-357.

Steinmetz, K.A. and Potter, J.D. Vegetables, fruit and cancer II. Mechanisms. *Cancer Causes and Control* (1991);2:427-442.

Steinmetz, K.A., et al. Vegetables, fruit and colon cancer in the Iowa Women's Health Study. *Am J Epidemiol* (1994);139:1-15.

Stephens, N.G., et al. Randomised controlled trial of vitamin E in patients with coronary disease: Cambridge Heart Antioxidant Study (CHAOS). *Lancet* (1996);347.

Taylor, A., et al. Relations among aging, antioxidant status, and cataract. *Am J Clin Nutr* (1995);62(suppl):1439S-1447S.

Thompson, L.U. Potential health benefits of whole grains and their components. Contemporary Nutrition (1992);17 (a General Mills publication).

Thun, M.J., et al. Risk factors for fatal colon cancer in a large prospective study. *J Nat Cancer Inst* (1992);84:1491-1500.

Thurnham, D.I. Carotenoids: function and fallacies. *Proc Nutr Soc* (1994); 53:77-87.

U.S. Department of Health and Human Services, Public Health Service, National Institutes of Health. National Cholesterol Education Program. *Cholesterol — Current Concepts for Clinicians,* 1988.

VERIS Vitamin E and Carotenoid Abstracts (1994).

Wang, H., et al. Total antioxidant capacity of fruits. *J Agric Food Chem* (1996);44:701-705.

Ward, J. Free radicals, antioxidants and preventive geriatrics. *Austr Family Phy* (1994);23:1297-1305.

Warshafsky, S., et al. Effect of garlic on total serum cholesterol. *Ann Intern Med* (1993);119:599-605.

Willett, W.C. Micronutrients and cancer risk. *Am J Clin Nutr* (1994);59(suppl):1162S-1165S.

Willett, W.C., et al. Relation of meat, fat and fiber intake to the risk of colon cancer in a prospective study among women. *N Engl J Med* (1990);323:1664-1672.

Zheng, W., et al. Retinol, antioxidant vitamins, and cancers of the upper digestive tract in a prospective cohort study of postmenopausal women. *Am J Epidemiol* (1995);142:955-959.

recipe index

science index

Order form

For telephone orders: Call toll-free 1-888-750-9336 or (214) 750-7322.

Have your MasterCard or Visa card ready.

Fax orders: (214) 750-7910

Online orders: www.phytopia.com

Postal orders: Phytopia Inc.,

       11705 Pine Forest Drive, Dallas, Texas 75230

❑ Please send me the Phytopia™ Newsletter

Please send *The Phytopia™ Cookbook* to:

Name: ....

Address: ....

City: .... State: .... Zip: ....

Telephone: (   ) ....

The Phytopia Cookbook (17.95 each)   ....

Sales tax: For books shipped to addresses in Texas, add 8.25% ....

Shipping: $4.^{00} for the first book and $2.^{00} for each additional book ....

Total: ....

Payment:

❑ Check

❑ Credit card: ❑ MasterCard ❑ Visa

Card number: ....

Name on card: ....exp. date: ....

Cardholder's Signature: ....

the
phytopia™
guarantee

If you're not completely satisfied with this cookbook, just return it with proof of purchase for a full refund.